CATWOMAN

THE VISUAL GUIDE TO THE FELINE FATALE

LONDON, NEW YORK, MELBOURNE,
MUNICH, AND DELHI

Senior Editor Alastair Dougall
Art Editor Nick Avery
Publishing Manager Cynthia O'Neill Collins
Publisher Alexandra Kirkham
Art Director Mark Richards
Production Nicola Torode
DTP Designer Dean Scholey

First American Edition, 2004

04 05 06 07 10 9 8 7 6 5 4 3 2 1

Published in the United States by DK Publishing, Inc.
375 Hudson Street, New York, New York 10014

DK Publishing, Inc. offers special discounts for bulk purchases for sales promotions or premiums.
Specific, large-quantity needs can be met with special editions, including personalized covers, excerpts
of existing guides, and corporate imprints. For more information, contact Special Markets Department,
DK Publishing, Inc., 375 Hudson Street, New York, NY 10014 Fax: 800-600-9098.

Published in Great Britain by Dorling Kindersley Limited.

A Cataloging-in-Publication record for this book is available from the Library of Congress.

ISBN 0-7566-0383-8

Color reproduction by Media Development and Printing Ltd., UK
Printed and bound in Italy by L.E.G.O.

Visit DC Comics online at www.dccomics.com
or at keyword DC Comics on America Online.

Discover more at
www.dk.com

CATWOMAN

THE VISUAL GUIDE TO THE FELINE FATALE

Written by Scott Beatty

CONTENTS

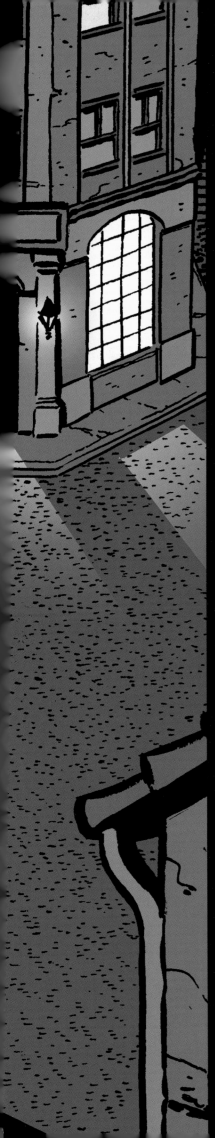

FOREWORD

I've always loved Catwoman as a character. From the very first time she appeared, as The Cat, she set herself apart from all the other Batman villains. She wasn't an insane murderer. She had style, class, brains, and just enough nerve to try to seduce the Dark Knight Detective. Over the years there have been a lot of different versions of Catwoman. My favorite incarnation as a kid was when she retired and married Bruce Wayne, and their daughter grew up to become the Huntress. I just really liked the idea that Selina Kyle wasn't necessarily bad, that her criminal side was just one part of her—an adventurous side, but not a murderous one. She never stole from anyone who couldn't afford it. No one ever went hungry because Catwoman stole a priceless artifact from a museum. She was like Robin Hood, except she forgot to give the money to the poor. And it was obvious Batman understood this, too, because he was always easier on her than on his other foes. So I thought the idea of them retiring and getting married was the perfect end to both their careers.

The grim 1980s brought us the beginning of the modern version of Selina Kyle, in Frank Miller's groundbreaking *Batman: Year One*. In just a few short scenes, Miller introduced a new Selina Kyle, one who had lived a hard life on the streets, could fight like the devil, and was inspired by the insanity of Batman and Gotham City to fashion a better life for herself and her friend Holly. It was a life less boring, but also one with a sense of justice. She robbed from the mobsters and the crooked politicians that had dragged her city down into the sewers. That version of Catwoman was so popular that she finally got her own comic book series, and she's been going strong ever since.

A few years ago, I was given the opportunity to write the Catwoman monthly series and to redefine her once more. My original collaborator, the talented Darwyn Cooke, even got to redesign her costume, based on a few notes and ideas I had come up with. I think the new look we ended up with was a great combination of classic and modern, which is something that perfectly describes Selina Kyle. This new version of Selina is a combination of the things I loved about the previous incarnations: the streetwise girl, the society girl, the thief with a heart, and the girl who Batman could love if she would just let him.

This book tells you all about her current life and mission, and introduces you to the cast of characters that surround her. It's humbling to be able to contribute to a popular character's story, especially one with such a long history. It's even more humbling to see your version detailed in a book like this.

Ed Brubaker

STYLE of the CAT

THAT FACE. That body. With or without a tail, Selina Kyle is one cat you'll never forget. Even in silhouette, the image of Catwoman is burned into the memories of those lucky—or unlucky—enough to cross her path in Gotham City. She seems to walk through walls and take whatever she wants. Then she's gone, roaring away into the night in her Kitty-Car or her Catplane, making tracks crouched over her Cat-Cycle, or springing away like a panther across the rooftops. While the cops scratch their heads and hunt for clues at the crime scene, Selina is tucked safely away in her secret lair or in a plush penthouse rented under an assumed name. And she's grinning like the Cheshire Cat while she toys with the pick of her loot, perhaps a priceless bauble fit for the one and only Princess of Plunder!

"The mask is part of who I am now. But it's also part of the problem, too…So, the question is, how to take back the mask…and still be able to live with myself."

Selina Kyle

CATWOMAN'S CATSUIT

FIRST THERE WAS LEATHER. Later came form-fitting spandex— in purple! Catwoman was an alluring sight to behold… but, as time passed, this sensuous, slinky style held too many bad associations for Selina Kyle. She felt she had strayed too far from the path that had initially led her to stalk the Gotham night. After a period in hiding, when many believed that she had died, Selina resolved to return as Catwoman. However, changing her life meant changing Catwoman's costume. Although it may be true that a leopard cannot change its spots, Selina aimed to prove that she was one cat who could. The *new* Catwoman would take full advantage of a feline's stealth and grace and ability to see better in the dark than most other creatures of the night. For her revamped costume, Selina took inspiration from woman aviators of the past, designing a leather jumpsuit and mask complete with night-vision goggles. Becoming Catwoman once more has given Selina a new lease on life, a chance to right the wrongs she has committed, and show that a cat in black isn't *always* bad luck.

Selina has cut her hair and opted for a low-maintenance hairstyle that only enhances her natural beauty.

Puss in boots

Aside from a few close allies, the world is unaware that Selina Kyle is Catwoman, which suits her just fine. Catwoman was inspired by Batman in the first place, so Selina was purring when the Dark Knight deemed her new catsuit "practical"—high praise from a man of so few words.

Crash helmet

Night-vision goggles

Choker collar

Catsuit assets

No animals were harmed in the making of Selina's high-tech imitation leather fighting gear, stolen from U.S. government surplus. Catwoman's costume is ideal for aerial acrobatics. Her "cat's-eye" goggles conceal her identity, glowing in the dark just like those of a true feline.

Police-band radio receiver in earpiece

Kevlar-reinforced padding

Catwoman's weapon of choice has always been a cat-o'-nine tails, its tip separated into nine metal-tipped tails for maximum flogging ability.

Retractable, razor-sharp claws

SENSIBLE SHOES

Catwoman's boots are fashionable and functional, as well as being ideal for rooftop adventures. Her footwear gives Catwoman sure footing on the narrowest of ledges. Spring-action titanium pitons in the toes of each boot offer additional purchase when scaling walls or clinging to speeding vehicles.

750,000-volt stun gun concealed within boot

Low-gloss imitation leather

10-foot-long, plaited cat-o'-nine-tails

A SCRATCH FROM THE CAT

"So Batman trailed me! Well, he'll learn that those who bother cats can get scratched!" Catwoman

THIS KITTEN has razor-sharp claws. And a biting whip. And vicious, steel climbing spikes in her boots. And that's just scratching the surface of all the feline fancy accoutrements Catwoman keeps in her arsenal. After the violent abuse she suffered as a child in juvenile detention, perhaps it is no surprise that Selina has developed something of a fetish for leather, and specifically the rawhide cat-o'-nine-tails that is now her signature accessory. But just as important to the intimidating image of the prowling Feline Fatale are the keen-edged claws she conceals in her gauntlets. And where would the most skillful cat burglar the world has ever known be without a supply of catnap powder in her kitty-compact to send savage watchdogs safely off to slumber?

While confined in the Sprang Hall Juvenile Detention Center, the snap of the cruel director's leather belt left a lasting impression on Selina.

Crack That Whip!

For young Selina, the crack of leather meant punishment. For Catwoman, the whip-snap of her preferred weapon reminds foes to keep away. In the hands of an expert like Selina, a leather bullwhip can snuff out the flame of a candle or flay flesh from bone in the blink of an eye.

Catwoman cracks her cat-o'-nine tails with its deadly weighted tips.

DUST OFF THOSE CROOKS FOR YOU!

MMMPPFF!

KOFF!

KOFF!

CHAK CHAK CHAK

The spring-loaded pitons in the toes of Catwoman's boots are more functional than fashionable.

Even without her cat-o'-nine-tails, Selina is one kitty who has never been declawed.

POWDER-PUFF GIRL

Anyone who expects to find catnip in the Feline Fatale's compact is in for a catnap instead when they get a whiff of her knockout powder. A puff can also be used to reveal hidden laser matrices in alarm systems.

SNEK

Claws of the Cat

An old adage attests: "A cat in gloves catches no mice." After reading those words, Selina modified her catsuit's gauntlets to house retractable claws for protection. Though trained in the use of edged weapons while a pupil at the Sensei's secret martial-arts dojo, Catwoman did not wish to be constricted by the scabbards or straps required to carry swords or sais. Besides, who could say no to ten two-inch blades available at the flick of a wrist? For cutting bonds, picking locks, or intimidating attackers, Catwoman's claws have served her well.

TOUGH AS NAILS

Forged from titanium, Catwoman's claws can pierce concrete or steel. But for climbing skyscrapers or catching hold of a speeding vehicle, the Feline Fatale's well-manicured nails are simply perfect.

With night-vision lenses enabling her to see in the dark, Catwoman is one dangerous predator.

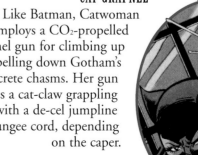

CAT-GRAPNEL

Like Batman, Catwoman employs a CO_2-propelled grapnel gun for climbing up or rappelling down Gotham's concrete chasms. Her gun features a cat-claw grappling hook with a de-cel jumpline or bungee cord, depending on the caper.

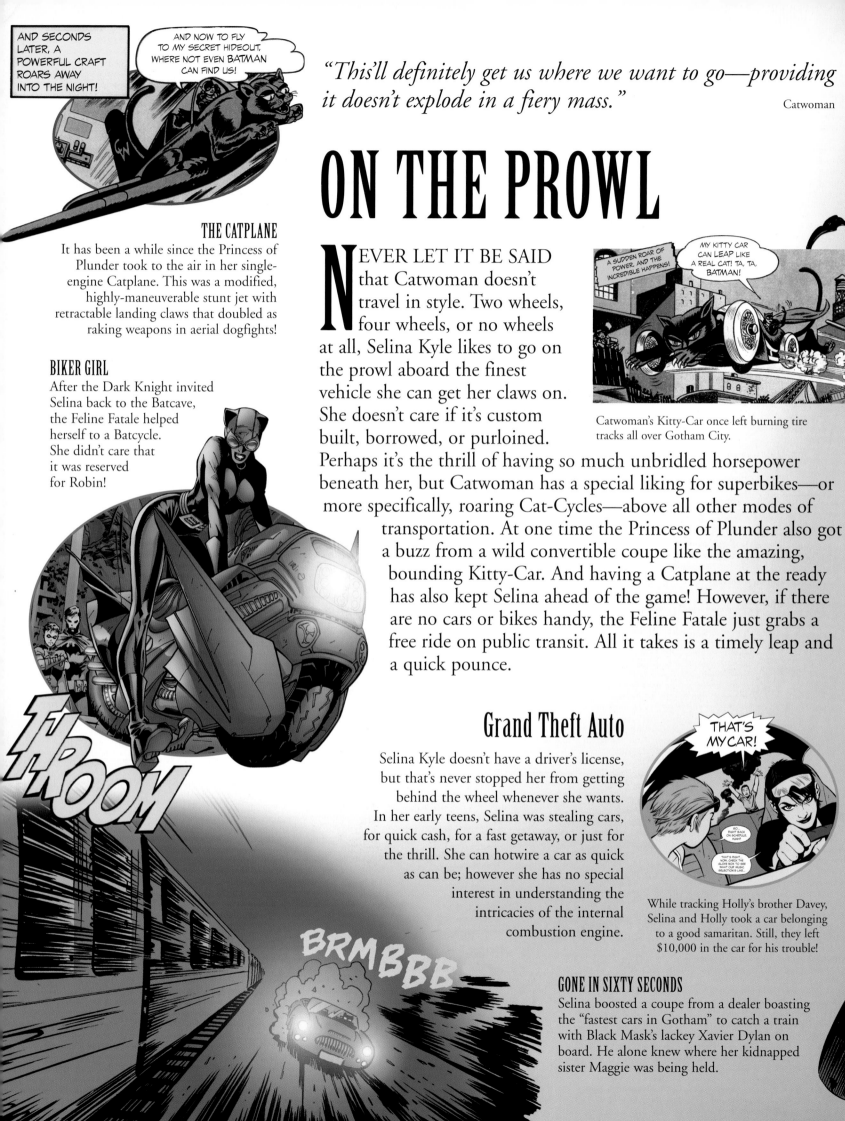

AND SECONDS LATER, A POWERFUL CRAFT ROARS AWAY INTO THE NIGHT!

AND NOW TO FLY TO MY SECRET HIDEOUT, WHERE NOT EVEN BATMAN CAN FIND US!

"This'll definitely get us where we want to go—providing it doesn't explode in a fiery mass."

Catwoman

ON THE PROWL

THE CATPLANE

It has been a while since the Princess of Plunder took to the air in her single-engine Catplane. This was a modified, highly-maneuverable stunt jet with retractable landing claws that doubled as raking weapons in aerial dogfights!

BIKER GIRL

After the Dark Knight invited Selina back to the Batcave, the Feline Fatale helped herself to a Batcycle. She didn't care that it was reserved for Robin!

NEVER LET IT BE SAID that Catwoman doesn't travel in style. Two wheels, four wheels, or no wheels at all, Selina Kyle likes to go on the prowl aboard the finest vehicle she can get her claws on. She doesn't care if it's custom built, borrowed, or purloined. Perhaps it's the thrill of having so much unbridled horsepower beneath her, but Catwoman has a special liking for superbikes—or more specifically, roaring Cat-Cycles—above all other modes of transportation. At one time the Princess of Plunder also got a buzz from a wild convertible coupe like the amazing, bounding Kitty-Car. And having a Catplane at the ready has also kept Selina ahead of the game! However, if there are no cars or bikes handy, the Feline Fatale just grabs a free ride on public transit. All it takes is a timely leap and a quick pounce.

A SUDDEN ROAR OF POWER, AND THE INCREDIBLE HAPPENS!

MY KITTY CAR CAN LEAP LIKE A REAL CAT! TA, TA, BATMAN!

Catwoman's Kitty-Car once left burning tire tracks all over Gotham City.

THROOM

BRMBBB

Grand Theft Auto

Selina Kyle doesn't have a driver's license, but that's never stopped her from getting behind the wheel whenever she wants. In her early teens, Selina was stealing cars, for quick cash, for a fast getaway, or just for the thrill. She can hotwire a car as quick as can be; however she has no special interest in understanding the intricacies of the internal combustion engine.

THAT'S MY CAR!

While tracking Holly's brother Davey, Selina and Holly took a car belonging to a good samaritan. Still, they left $10,000 in the car for his trouble!

GONE IN SIXTY SECONDS

Selina boosted a coupe from a dealer boasting the "fastest cars in Gotham" to catch a train with Black Mask's lackey Xavier Dylan on board. He alone knew where her kidnapped sister Maggie was being held.

Cat-Cycle

The Cat's favorite ride was a super-fast prototype she filched that featured a silent-running stealth mode. Selina's admiring armorer Clutterbuck fitted the bike with a custom cat-canopy and tuned its high-tech fuel injectors to a fine purr.

It's crash and burn time when Catwoman won't give way to an oncoming Batmobile! Luckily, it wasn't *her* car!

GETTING AROUND

These days Catwoman prefers to keep a low profile. Instead of tooling around town on hot wheels, she's more likely to hitch a free ride on top of one of Gotham City's elevated trains.

GOTHAM HTS

2688

C

Selina enters her lair through a remote-controlled skylight.

LAIRS OF THE CAT

"[I] bought this place back in the early days to be a sanctuary… a secret home away from the street and the life."

Selina Kyle

FOLLOWERS OF CATWOMAN'S exploits might imagine that the Queen of Crime plans her heists in some high-tech hideout. They might think she possesses a "Catacombs" lair to rival the Dark Knight's Batcave, filled with feline *objets d'art* and carpeted in stolen cash. Think again: Selina began life in a slum and clawed her way to the top to live in a luxury penthouse. She doesn't have much interest in personal possessions any more. Nowadays, Selina's digs at the end of Lark Street in Gotham's East End are filled with just enough creature comforts to make a Princess of Plunder feel at home. However this alley cat is quite prepared to live out of a suitcase in an abandoned tenement if the heat is on!

Selina rarely names her pet cats unless they stick around long enough to reveal their true personalities, and that includes the felines she's dubbed "Sleepy" and "Lazy."

Home Body

Because Catwoman works the "night shift," she often sleeps late and relaxes in the afternoon with a cup of coffee—Sumatra when she's in, Mint Mocha when she's out and about—and the *Gotham Gazette* (Her favorite section is The Crime Beat). She also keeps a scrapbook of her "greatest hits."

16

Before she became Catwoman, Selina shared a rundown flat with her friend Holly Robinson and just about every stray cat prowling the East End.

BE IT EVER SO HUMBLE...

Selina currently lives in a modest building in the East End. Holly is once again her roommate. While they don't share the same tastes (in *anything*, really), Holly doesn't complain too loudly when Selina wants to relax by listening to some Billie Holiday or Miles Davis. However, Holly would prefer something a little more contemporary than Sly Stone or early Brian Eno when she joins Selina's rigorous workout regimen of aerobics, yoga, and Pilates.

With her "thing" for leather, it's no surprise that Selina enjoys listening to vinyl. She just likes the scratch and hiss of the needle on a record album.

OTHER DENS

Selina likes to keep her home life and "work" separate, but sometimes pursuers threaten to compromise her lair. So she maintains "bolt holes" all over the neighborhood and throughout Gotham. These homes away from home contain various disguises and changes of clothes, as well as spare catsuits and emergency supplies.

BEWARE OF THE CAT!

Who needs a sophisticated home-security system when you've got a big cat to scare off even the most fearless of intruders? Although private ownership of a black panther isn't strictly legal, that didn't stop Selina from keeping one in her Park Row apartment. Tame only to his mistress's touch, Diablo didn't care for strangers—Batman especially—invading his territory!

MIND of the CAT

JUST WHO IS Selina Kyle? That's the thing about Selina. You just never know… unless she wants you to. And cats are capricious with whom they keep company. Selina prefers anonymity. Growing up on the wrong side of the tracks after losing everyone she ever loved, she had to do some unsavory things to survive. Prideful and private, Selina is a work-in-progress, adapting to adversity. And Catwoman? Well, having a secret identity is contingent upon *keeping* it a secret. Otherwise, Selina might just as well wear a neon sign proclaiming that she's the Princess of Plunder! No, that's one bit of information she'll keep under her cat mask. Aside from a few friends and lovers, Selina and Catwoman are two different women moving in different worlds. And that suits them both just fine. Because when those two worlds collide, somebody almost always gets hurt… or killed.

Could this victimized backstreet prostitute be the real Selina Kyle?

"She is a loner, a thief, a creature of the night and shadows. She is a cat… and she is a woman. But once… once, she was a child."

Anonymous

Could this gorgeous Gotham socialite be the real Selina Kyle?

WHO IS SELINA?

T O UNDERSTAND the tangled complexity of Selina Kyle, alias Catwoman, one must first examine her traumatic childhood. Selina's upbringing played a huge role in forming her personality. She was raised in poverty and in an atmosphere of fear and uncertainty. From the first she was made to feel guilty, inferior. Witnessing her mother's abuse at the hands of her unemployed, alcoholic father and later seeing *both* her parents die before her very eyes would surely have torn apart a weaker individual. But somehow these bitter experiences made Selina stronger and more determined to escape destitution and misery.

Selina's mother desperately tried to shield her daughters from Brian Kyle's alcohol-fueled abuse.

THE SINS OF THE FATHER

Brian Kyle may once have been a good man, but alcohol unleashed his inner demons. Selina and her younger sister Magdalena escaped the worst of Brian's wrath, but their mother did not. His explosive rages drove Maria Kyle to suicide. Overcome with remorse, Brian drank himself to death. The orphaned children were split up and sent to juvenile wards; it would be years before Selina and Maggie would see each other again.

> **NOBODY HURTS HOLLY...**

> THIS SUIT WAS BUILT BY COLLEGE GEEKS WHO WANTED TO TAKE A TRIP INTO THE HEART OF AN ACTIVE VOLCANO.

> GOOD IDEA, HOLLY. TURNING THE SUIT AROUND SO THE TETHERED LINE ATTACHMENT BECOMES A TAIL.

> I DON'T KNOW, SELINA-- I MEAN, YOU SPENT ALL OUR *MONEY* ON THAT COSTUME...

> IT'S *MONEY*, HOLLY. IT GROWS ON TREES.

HEADING FOR THE MEAN STREETS

Aged 13, Selina escaped the Sprang Hall Juvenile Detention Center and made her way back to Gotham City. There, the runaway lived by her wits. By the time she was 17, Selina dwelt in relative comfort in Gotham's crime-ridden East End, where she befriended a young prostitute, Holly Robinson. Selina took to defending Holly and other East End streetwalkers.

FISTFIGHT

It was here that Selina first met Bruce Wayne, before he became Batman. The would-be vigilante got into a scuffle with Selina after trying to protect Holly from her pimp.

In the beginning, Holly was the only person who knew Selina's secret identity.

Costumed for Crime

If not for Batman, there might never have been a Catwoman. Witnessing the Dark Knight in action was an inspiring moment for Selina Kyle. If he could be a bat, why shouldn't she be a cat? Batman's frightening outfit seemed to gave him an almost mythic power, and Selina was confident that a costumed Catwoman would soon fill her empty purse with purloined prizes.

PREYING ON THE PREDATORS

When not looking out for Holly and the East Enders, Selina pursued a career as a cat burglar. "The Cat" usually preyed on the even more predatory politicians and crooked businessmen who used and abused Holly and the East End girls. In a way, Selina was simply exploiting those who exploited Gotham's castoffs.

Living the Dream

Catwoman made Selina Kyle rich, and she emerged into Gotham's elite social circles as a young and beautiful lady of leisure. With no living relatives to reveal her past, Selina moved easily among the wealthy and famous. The poor girl from Gotham's slums was now a pampered princess… of plunder.

> DOES MADEMOISELLE NEED ANOTHER *DRINK*?

> SHE SEEMS TO HAVE FALLEN ASLEEP. I WOULD NOT DISTURB HER UNLESS SHE STARTS TO *BURN*.

SHEER CLASS
Selina's mother encouraged her daughter's amazing gymnastic talent. Later, the orphaned Selina demonstrated her catlike agility in the exercise yard at the Sprang Hall Juvenile Detention Center.

ENOUGH OF THAT, KYLE-- FEET ON THE GROUND!

"See, I've got what Sensei's called incredible hand-eye coordination and physical memory. That means I see a move once and I've got it for LIFE."

Selina Kyle

POWERS OF THE CAT

SHE POSSESSES no superpowers, but Selina Kyle's unique upbringing shaped her into an agile athlete and highly capable hand-to-hand combatant. While still a child, Selina learned to steal. To live well she had to steal well. And in Gotham City—an urban jungle where only the fittest survive—the kitten who would become Catwoman learned how to fight tooth and nail to protect herself and her freedom. Gifted with an uncanny sense of balance and a fiercely independent streak, Selina mastered martial arts and escapology so that she would never again be caged.

For Selina, liberation from Sprang Hall meant scaling high ledges and springing over steep rooftops!

En garde!

She prefers a cat-o'-nine-tails, but Catwoman is handy with virtually any weapon. Prince Willem Kapreallian vainly hoped to wed Selina and thought he could best his bride-to-be in swordplay. Catwoman showed the Transbelvian ruler that she was as sharp with an épée as with her own claws.

A TIGER BY THE TAIL
In a fight, Selina's will to win makes her a howling hellcat able to claw her way out of almost any scrape. Even when overwhelmed and outnumbered, she never turns tail before drawing first blood!

VANISHING CAT

Selina is so lightning quick that not even a stakeout by Gotham's Finest can ensnare her. In just seconds she's cartwheeling to freedom down a dark backstreet.

Hard Target

Catwoman isn't bulletproof, and neither is her costume. Her catsuit provides complete freedom of movement, which means no bulky Kevlar padding. Selina makes up for this lack of armor with stealth and speed, dodging gunshots with acrobatics that guarantee she always lands on her feet!

The Sensei

Young Selina Kyle seemed to have bitten off more than she could chew when she burgled her way into a secret Gotham karate dojo. Although outnumbered twenty-to-one, Selina stood her ground ready to fight. Her boldness and grace under pressure greatly impressed the fight club's charismatic chief instructor, the armless Sensei. Selina soon became his star pupil, an honor previously held by the arrogant Kai. Selina easily bested Kai. The future Hellhound never forgot this humiliation.

KNOCKOUT PUNCH

Selina has always been tough. However, she was taught to punch far above her weight by Ted Grant, an ex-heavyweight boxing champ and occasional costumed hero known as Wildcat. Grant taught her all he knew about the "sweet science."

Catwoman packs a punch with both fists! After staggering rival rogue the Catman with a left-jab, Selina knocked him silly with her paw-knuckle strike!

BAKT!

CAT CUNNING

"It was a great plan while it lasted." Catwoman

SEE...ALL THE OPALESCENT REFLECTIONS FROM WITHIN... SEE HOW IT WINKS LIKE A CAT'S EYE...

CLOSER, CLOSER THE **CATWOMAN** BRINGS THE STRANGE CRYSTAL! HER VOICE BECOMES SOFT, DEEP, THROBBING—A CAT'S PURR!

Selina mesmerized her prison guard with a cat's-eye gem to make a jailbreak!

ASK ANY SUCCESSFUL cat burglar and they'll tell you it's all in the planning. Selina Kyle rapidly evolved from a snatch-and-grab thief to a stealthy cat burglar in just a few years. Selina's smarts have never been in short supply, which is why she has rarely been captured and caged. For her, knowledge and preparedness are the keys to staying one step ahead of the law. Before she even begins a heist, it's better than even money that she has plotted several exit strategies.

PEEPING CAT
Selina wouldn't even dream of breaking and entering until she has familiarized herself with the layout—peeping under doors and around corners with her flexible, fiberoptic spy-scope.

DOGS' BREAKFAST
The Feline Fatale could certainly do without the wearisome worry of watchdogs in the grounds of wealthy estates or roaming around high-security facilities. These doggies got a special treat…

…prime rib steaks laced with knockout catnip!

Brains and Beauty

As a child, Selina was diagnosed as having a learning disability because she used to fail one exam while earning perfect marks in another. None of her teachers suspected that schoolwork often bored Selina—nor that her amazing problem-solving skills would be ideally suited to a career in cat burglary!

"You make your own luck in this business"—Selina's mind is as sharp as her claws.

Manhunter

When Warner Samson's lust for Selina strayed close to stalking, she decided to give him a taste of his own scare tactics. Like a predator watching its prey, Selina observed the lewd Lothario's every move, studying his habits, infiltrating his haunts. Selina even went so far as to become Samson's golf caddy and fitness instructor for a day. Still, not a bad way to have your privacy invaded!

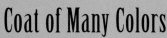

Coat of Many Colors

Dressed up or dressed down, Selina Kyle is one cat that knows the value of camouflage. Raven-haired, elegant, and evening-gowned, she drew gasps in Gotham dining with billionaire Bruce Wayne. Trailing a serial killer, she became a bodacious blonde barfly in thigh-high boots. Amid the neon glitz of Las Vegas, she was a razzle-dazzling redhead in a tube-top who turned heads as she catwalked through the casinos!

WHIP SMART

Catwoman's preference for a cat-o'-nine-tails may seem strange, but her whip is both an offensive and defensive weapon, a convenient grapple and a line to swing by, and more! With a deft flick, she caught Poison Ivy's deadly phial and, with a snap of her wrist, planted a smacking kiss Ivy wouldn't forget!

Nine Lives?

Selina definitely has nine lives considering the number of times she has survived near-fatal catastrophes. Luck was certainly with her when she walked away from this not-so-happy landing as she attempted to penetrate the "No Man's Land" of Gotham City by helicopter.

THOOM

"Relationships have never been easy for me. It's always been easier—SAFER—to keep people at a distance."

Selina Kyle

FRIENDS AND FAMILY

SELINA MAY STRUT like a stray cat, aloof and alone, but even this fiercely independent feline sometimes craves companionship. In the many years since her parents' deaths, Selina has found people to replace the family she tragically lost. The orphaned sisters, Selina and Magdalena Kyle, were forced apart during their time in Gotham City's child welfare system. Unfortunately, reconnecting in adulthood led to tragedy for Maggie. Perhaps that's why Selina has always been so protective of Holly Robinson, the little sister she never had. Ted Grant, the former boxing champ who taught Selina self-defense, has been more of a father to her than alcoholic Brian Kyle ever was. And whether or not she'll admit it, Selina appreciates Dr. Leslie Thompkins worrying over her as only a mother would.

PERMIT ME TO INTRODUCE MYSELF! I AM THE MASTER OF THE CAT KINGDOM...THE **KING OF THE CATS!**

Rumor has it that Selina once had a big brother, a criminal called Catman!

HOLLY AND SELINA

On the streets of Gotham's East End, Holly was once known as "Holly Gonightly," a drug-addicted runaway from a troubled home who would do whatever she had to do to survive. While in her teens, Selina protected Holly as best she could. The pair lost touch for several years, but recently rekindled their friendship. Selina helped Holly to finally kick her drug dependency and and, like Selina's alter ego Catwoman, reinvent herself for the better.

Bad Luck and Trouble

Selina's sister Maggie became Sister Magdalena of the Gotham Catholic Diocese. After being briefly reunited with Selina, Maggie left the church and, with Holly Robinson in tow, stole a car and drove to San Francisco. She earned a college degree in psychology and married computer expert Simon Burton. However, gang boss Black Mask, out for revenge against Catwoman, tortured Simon to death before Maggie's eyes.

The Wild One

In 1942, heavyweight boxer Ted Grant was falsely accused of murdering an opponent. He was inspired by the exploits of Green Lantern to clear his name by battling the criminals who framed him. He became the hard-hitting "Mystery Man" Wildcat.

FLANNERY WAS RIGHT. YOU DON'T KNOW ANYTHING ABOUT FIGHTING.

ANIMAL MAGNETISM

Ted taught Selina how to fight, and he was a hard taskmaster. Although they have never acted upon it, there is definitely a certain animal attraction there, despite the age difference!

MEMORIES OF MAGGIE

During one of her encounters with Batman's arch-foe the Scarecrow, Catwoman was injected with psychotropic drugs and given post-hypnotic suggestions that triggered her childhood fears. As the Scarecrow's mind games preyed upon her, Selina struggled to remember that her sister Maggie had ever existed!

A FRIEND INDEED

Physician Leslie Thompkins has a soft spot for Selina and helps her and also her friends, such as Holly, whenever she can at her free clinic in Gotham's "Crime Alley."

CATWOMAN VS. BATMAN

> JUST BECAUSE I LET YOU KISS ME --
>
> --DOESN'T MEAN YOU GET TO TREAT ME LIKE YOUR TOY WONDER.

For the Cat and the Bat, the line between love and hate has always been paper thin.

"A weird one, all right, but who am I to talk? Hell, we'd make the perfect pair… two of the dark ones, drawing down the Gotham moon… with our HOWLS."

Catwoman

> BLACK HAIR IS REVEALED UNDER THE GREY WIG!
>
> FIRST--OFF WITH THE WIG!
>
> YOU-- YOU--!!

UNMASKED
Catwoman no longer had the upper paw when Batman peeled away her dowager disguise to reveal svelte, sly Selina. Perhaps, deep down, the Cat *wanted* to get caught.

From the moment they first met, the attraction was obvious. However, crucial differences in temperament always pulled Catwoman and the Dark Knight apart after the passionate rooftop embraces that so often concluded their breathless chases. After all, he had dedicated himself to fighting an unrelenting war on crime, while she prided herself on being Gotham City's charismatic cat burglar. To Batman then, Catwoman was a criminal to be caught and caged, like any other. Or was she? She was not a homicidal horror like the Joker. She didn't advertise her thefts with pranking puzzles like the Riddler. No, her heists were smaller, more personal. And since insurance companies would invariably cover the costs of whatever she stole, Selina considered her scores "victimless" offenses. Batman didn't. But could he ever persuade her to change her ways?

> IS THIS WHAT YOU REALLY WANT!

Friend or Foe?

The Dark Knight would have preferred to spend his patrols hunting *real* predators. But Commissioner Gordon pressured Batman to stop treating the Feline Fatale with kid gloves. If the Caped Crusader couldn't catch the Cat, Gotham's Finest would… and with far less restraint.

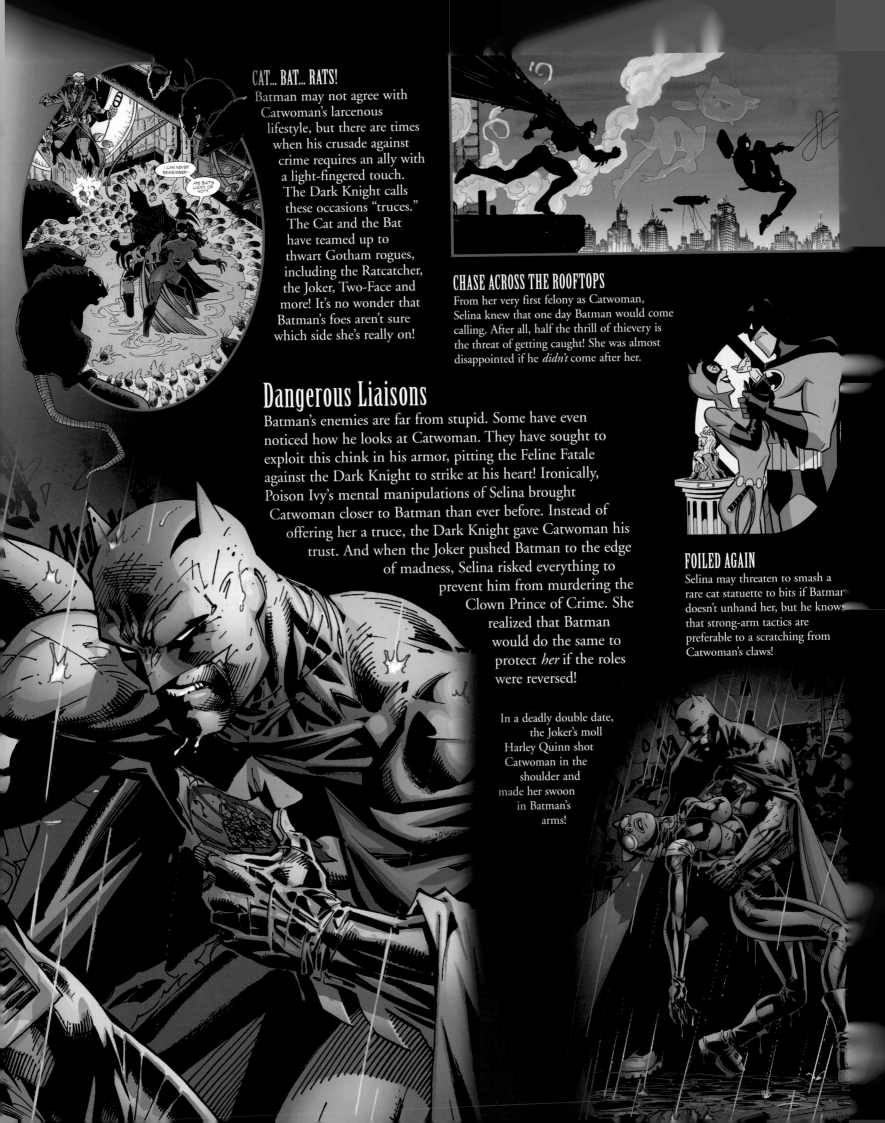

CAT... BAT... RATS!

Batman may not agree with Catwoman's larcenous lifestyle, but there are times when his crusade against crime requires an ally with a light-fingered touch. The Dark Knight calls these occasions "truces." The Cat and the Bat have teamed up to thwart Gotham rogues, including the Ratcatcher, the Joker, Two-Face and more! It's no wonder that Batman's foes aren't sure which side she's really on!

CHASE ACROSS THE ROOFTOPS

From her very first felony as Catwoman, Selina knew that one day Batman would come calling. After all, half the thrill of thievery is the threat of getting caught! She was almost disappointed if he *didn't* come after her.

Dangerous Liaisons

Batman's enemies are far from stupid. Some have even noticed how he looks at Catwoman. They have sought to exploit this chink in his armor, pitting the Feline Fatale against the Dark Knight to strike at his heart! Ironically, Poison Ivy's mental manipulations of Selina brought Catwoman closer to Batman than ever before. Instead of offering her a truce, the Dark Knight gave Catwoman his trust. And when the Joker pushed Batman to the edge of madness, Selina risked everything to prevent him from murdering the Clown Prince of Crime. She realized that Batman would do the same to protect *her* if the roles were reversed!

In a deadly double date, the Joker's moll Harley Quinn shot Catwoman in the shoulder and made her swoon in Batman's arms!

FOILED AGAIN

Selina may threaten to smash a rare cat statuette to bits if Batman doesn't unhand her, but he knows that strong-arm tactics are preferable to a scratching from Catwoman's claws!

DOOR JAMMED--!

HAVE TO PULL YOU THROUGH THE *WINDOW*!

CAN'T HOLD MY *BREATH* MUCH LONGER--HARD TO *FOCUS*--!

KRASSH!

CATWOMAN!

NOT TAKING ANY *CHANCES*, ARE YOU!

YOU WANT TO MAKE *SURE* SHE'S *FINISHED*!

HOW COULD I EVER HAVE THOUGHT I *LOVED* YOU?

CAT LOVES BAT

MMMMMMM

I WAS BEGINNING TO THINK YOU INTENDED TO SLEEP *FOREVER*!

Selina awakes after a night in the Batcave—a rare moment of calm in the lives of Gotham City's most passionate pair.

"Forget about being a detective just once. We are who we are. That's why this works. Maybe someday, you'll come to trust THAT." Catwoman to Batman

IT WASN'T LOVE at first sight, but it might have come a close second... Batman inspired Selina Kyle to don her catsuit and stalk the Gotham night as Catwoman.

Their paths were destined to cross, and not just in a clash of claws. Soon, inspiration would inevitably give way to powerful attraction. From the beginning, Catwoman enjoyed the chase—he chasing *her*, that is. Batman wanted to reform the Feline Fatale. Catwoman wanted to know the man behind the cowl. And in time, the Cat and the Bat acted on their feelings, but only after Selina convinced the Dark Knight that she was worthy of him by upholding the law instead of breaking it. Broken hearts, however, are another story…

Catwoman uses the Bat-Signal, a police method of contacting Batman, to plan a midnight rendezvous.

FATAL ATTRACTION

In another time and place, passions ran high when Selina discovered boyfriend Bruce Wayne canoodling in his limo with old flame Vicki Vale. Selina did what any Feline Fatale would do—she ran them off the road!

*...N WE FINALLY HOOKED UP AND
...MED OUR USUAL RELATIONSHIP?
...BAT ASKED ME FOR A FAVOR?*

I HAVE NEED OF A THIEF.

THERE ARE SOME COMPUTER DISKS THAT CONTAIN VITAL DATA FOR RESTORING GOTHAM.

THEY'RE IN MANHATTAN.

LOVE WILL TEAR THEM APART

Catwoman stole kisses from the Dark Knight before she stole his heart. To win him over, she had to earn his trust. Batman suspected that Catwoman was more altruistic than she ever let on. He enlisted Catwoman's aid on several missions and witnessed her willingness to risk her life for the future of Gotham City, and for him. Batman revealed his true identity to Catwoman, demonstrating his love for her. Yet each time they seem to be becoming closer than ever before, he pushes Catwoman away.

In Catwoman's dream, a bevy of superheroines started a catfight during the bouquet toss!

NO WAY.

I HAVE TO RESPOND. GOTHAM NEEDS ME.

TO HELL WITH GOTHAM. I OWN YOU NOW.

YOU UNDERSTOOD THIS BEFORE WE WERE MARRIED.

I HAVE *COMMITMENTS*, SELINA.

What Might Have Been...

A dream may herald waking desire... Selina dreamed that she and Batman were wed while Gotham's super heroes and rogues cheered. But just as the happy couple were about to depart on their honeymoon, duty called the Dark Knight to action. No wife would stand for that, of course, and Selina was no exception: out came the whip! But could this dream *ever* come true?

KRAK

FWISHT!

YOU SURE DO, BUCKO.

TO ME

Was Bruce ashamed, or worried that his secret identity would be jeopardized by his romance with Catwoman?

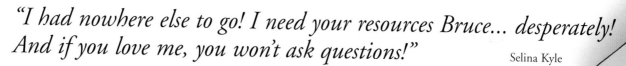

"I had nowhere else to go! I need your resources Bruce... desperately! And if you love me, you won't ask questions!"

Selina Kyle

SELINA AND BRUCE

OUT OF COSTUME, their relationship is different, certainly less violent and explosive, yet still fraught with unresolved sexual tension. But that was when Selina Kyle and Bruce Wayne thought each other to be wealthy Gotham socialites, a perfect match according to the high-society gossip columns—he the billionaire bachelor playboy and she the gorgeous *ingénue*. For a short while, the alter egos of Catwoman and Batman separately believed that this new love would offer their costumed aliases a reason to hang up their capes and cowls, perhaps settle down for good. But that was before the Dark Knight learned Selina Kyle's secret. And later, when Batman unmasked himself before Catwoman, both knew that they were either destined to be together… or too much alike for their love to endure.

THE OTHER WOMAN

All's fair in love and war… but not where the Dark Knight's war on crime is concerned. Could Bruce force Catwoman to choose between him and a life of crime without revealing he was—in costume, at least—her greatest foe?

DREAMING HER DREAMS

Through thievery, Catwoman met Batman. She also made herself over as a rich playgirl. That role was just another mask, but Selina couldn't help dreaming about how life could be as Mrs. Bruce Wayne, protected, cosseted, *loved for herself...* Was that sort of happiness so far-fetched, so *out of reach?*

LA VIE EN ROSE

Bruce Wayne's billionaire lifestyle was an important part of his appeal for Selina—at first. Most of the women Bruce dated couldn't get past his bored playboy exterior, but Selina saw through this carefully constructed façade, sensing that there was much more to him than met the eye.

VALENTINE'S NIGHT. SELINA KYLE.

CUT YOURSELF SHAVING, BRUCE?

HMMM?

YOUR LIP. YOU SHOULD HAVE SOMEONE DO THAT FOR YOU.

ALFRED HAS OFFERED MORE THAN ONCE.

PASSION PLAY

Recently, Selina learned that the men she was torn between—Bruce Wayne and Batman—were one and the same! As the Dark Knight was attacked from all sides—the villain Hush setting Batman's worst foes against him—Bruce turned to Selina for help, trusting her as never before. In the end, however, the emotionally ravaged Dark Knight was unable to trust his own feelings and pushed Catwoman away.

"I thought that would be it… just two friends comforting each other. But it didn't turn out that way."

Selina Kyle

CAT LOVERS

For the love of Selina, Slam saved Holly from a hit and run driver!

L UCKY IN LOVE is something Selina Kyle has never been. Her strange relationship with the Dark Knight hardly qualifies as a fairy-tale romance. More accurately, it's an "inter-species" affair with all the expected incompatibilities. But cats aren't monogamous… usually. And when the Cat and Bat aren't casting furtive glances at each other from across moonlit rooftops, Selina doesn't sit around in her lair waiting for him to call. As time has gone by, she has had other lovers. Some, such as her affair with private eye Slam Bradley, have ended in mutual friendship. But there are a few failed flings, including being stalked by serial killer Moreland McShane, that she'd just as soon forget!

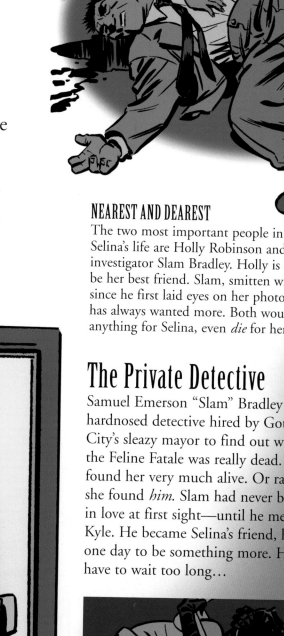

NEAREST AND DEAREST

The two most important people in Selina's life are Holly Robinson and private investigator Slam Bradley. Holly is content to be her best friend. Slam, smitten with Selina since he first laid eyes on her photograph, has always wanted more. Both would do anything for Selina, even *die* for her.

The Private Detective

Samuel Emerson "Slam" Bradley was the hardnosed detective hired by Gotham City's sleazy mayor to find out whether the Feline Fatale was really dead. Slam found her very much alive. Or rather, she found *him*. Slam had never believed in love at first sight—until he met Selina Kyle. He became Selina's friend, hoping one day to be something more. He didn't have to wait too long…

NIGHT CALLER

Slam Bradley figured out soon enough that he could have Selina, but not hold onto her heart. He had seen enough jealous types in his line of work to know that romances like that only end badly. At the end of their brief affair, the two parted as friends.

Stark knew that nobody could ever own Selina. But he could never resist her charms...

The Career Criminal

Selina thought of Stark as "living granite." He was the killer who kicked her door in and shot Tony "The Toucan" Tudeska in cold blood right before her eyes. Stark taught her how to think big where crime was concerned. They shared a kind of love, but Selina suspected that Stark was loyal to nobody but Stark. So she snatched $500,000 in diamonds from him. When they met again years later, Stark might have killed her if she hadn't offered him an even bigger score to make up for stealing his stones. He should have known better than to let a black cat cross his path *twice*.

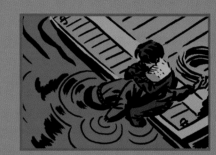

Long-repressed emotions surfaced as Stark died in Selina's arms.

The Serial Killer

Commissioner Gordon of the G.C.P.D. never expected romantic entanglements when he assigned Detective Moreland McShane to ensnare Catwoman! When McShane got too close, the Cat scratched and scarred his cheeks to scare him off. She never thought that she'd fall head-over-heels for the handsome young cop! Soon the cat was out of the bag when McShane figured out that the two women he was pursuing, Selina Kyle and the Catwoman, were the same person! But sometimes secrets cut both ways, never more so than when Selina discovered that Moreland led his *own* double-life: as the serial slayer known as the Headhunter!

The Headhunter wanted more than a trophy girlfriend... he wanted Selina's skull!

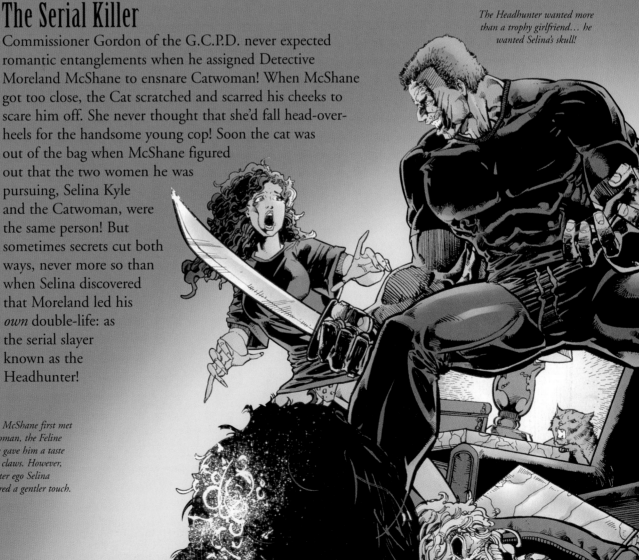

When McShane first met Catwoman, the Feline Fatale gave him a taste of her claws. However, her alter ego Selina preferred a gentler touch.

CRIMES of the CAT

SHE HAS A THING for cats and she has bills to pay like anyone else. So chances are that Catwoman will give any feline-shaped antique jade figurine or gold statuette more than a passing glance. She also has a taste for priceless paintings, though they can be hard to unload in an art market that's thick with thieves. There's always industrial espionage, satisfying to Selina because she enjoys stealing from ruthless robber barons. And of course she is always on the lookout for that really big score, the heist that could set her up for life. At other times, Selina's unauthorized withdrawals have caused her to work on the *right* side of the law, for a while even keeping company with super heroes! Unfortunately, being a fence-sitter on the thin line separating good from evil doesn't make her a neutral party. These days Selina seems to have enemies on *both* sides, none of whom take too kindly to her light-fingered ways.

RAISED ON ROBBERY

"How do I steal enough to make it felt? So that it will be noticed? So that it HURTS?"

Catwoman

STEALING BIG or stealing small, Selina Kyle has done it all. At first, it was steal or starve. Petty theft put food in her belly and clothes on her back. Later, Selina's kleptomania improved her station in life. Unselfishly, she shared her spoils with the unfortunate of Gotham's underprivileged East End. That streak of good in Selina runs deep, especially when she robs the deep-pocketed rich and gives a goodly portion to the needy. But sometimes the heist is just for *her*, stealing something pretty or priceless to scratch an itch only a poor orphaned girl like Selina Kyle could ever understand.

SMASH AND GRAB

Early on, Selina was reckless in her robberies. Smashing a jeweler's window and grabbing fistfuls of diamonds and pearls. Selina artfully dodged bullets and later pawned the "ice" for cold hard cash.

CAT BURGLARY

When Selina had no one else for support, she could always count on a stray cat to stroke her ego. Perhaps that's why she's so attracted to feline finery. Catwoman couldn't resist heisting an ancient cat icon carved from pure jade. However, replacing the mystical Manx back upon its altar seemed like the right thing to do, until the figurine's eldritch energies shocked Selina senseless!

Selina overrode the robots' programming and triggered them to steal for her!

Remote-control Robbers

Selina left Gotham for a cleaner litter box when the city was hit by an earthquake. Batman, however, lured her back to her hometown, now a lawless No Man's Land. Working as the Dark Knight's ally, Catwoman copped vital computer disks from Metropolis Mogul Lex Luthor that ultimately helped to reopen and rebuild Gotham. Selina also looted Luthor's resources. Slinking into a bulletproof battlesuit, a flying Feline Fatale stole Luthor's army of robots to aid and abet her deconstruction of LexCorp!

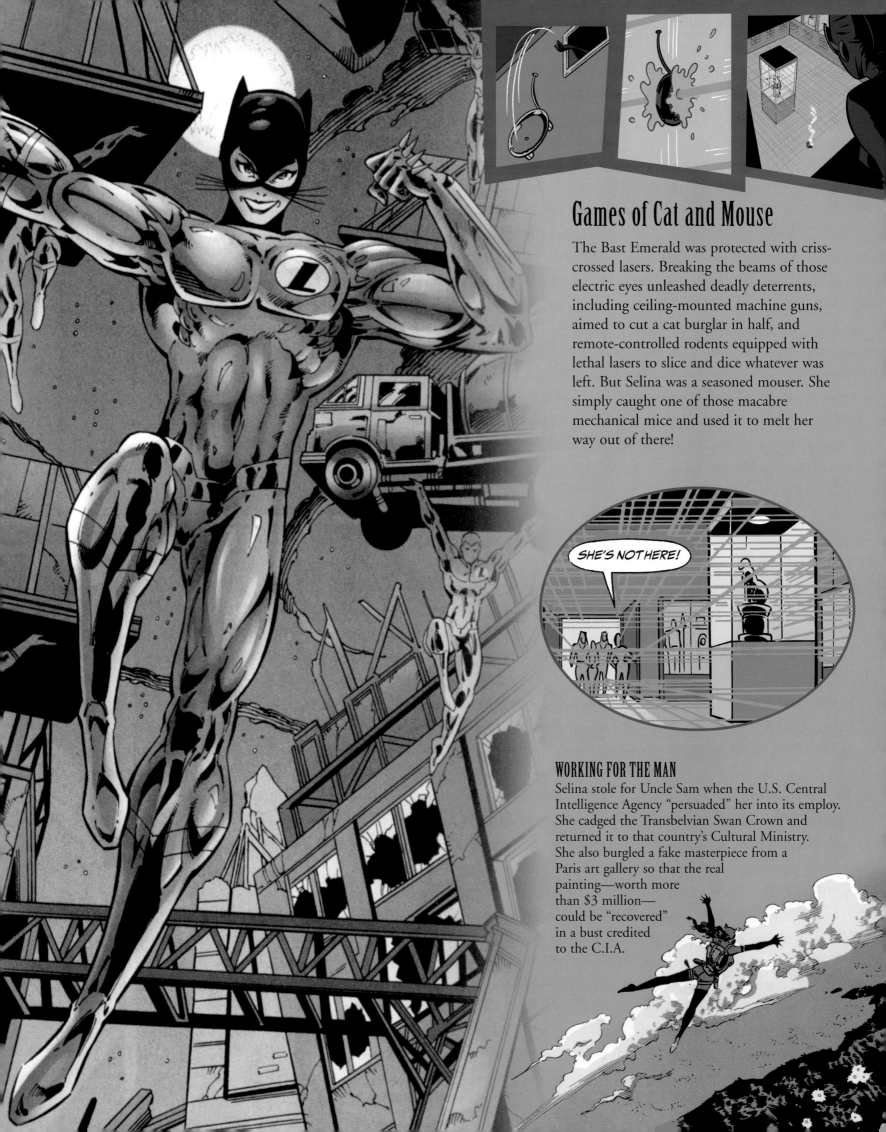

Games of Cat and Mouse

The Bast Emerald was protected with criss-crossed lasers. Breaking the beams of those electric eyes unleashed deadly deterrents, including ceiling-mounted machine guns, aimed to cut a cat burglar in half, and remote-controlled rodents equipped with lethal lasers to slice and dice whatever was left. But Selina was a seasoned mouser. She simply caught one of those macabre mechanical mice and used it to melt her way out of there!

SHE'S NOT HERE!

WORKING FOR THE MAN

Selina stole for Uncle Sam when the U.S. Central Intelligence Agency "persuaded" her into its employ. She cadged the Transbelvian Swan Crown and returned it to that country's Cultural Ministry. She also burgled a fake masterpiece from a Paris art gallery so that the real painting—worth more than $3 million—could be "recovered" in a bust credited to the C.I.A.

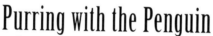

Selina collaborated with Captain Cold to break into the Keystone City Time Capsule Memorial and steal away with a helmet that belonged to the original Flash, Jay Garrick.

"I'm just now remembering that you're a stickler for working alone. Prefer an edge of ANIMOSITY in your relationships, don't you?"

The Trickster

PARTNERS IN CRIME

CATS ARE SOLITARY CREATURES and Selina Kyle is no exception. Ever since she first embarked on a career in cat-burglary, the Princess of Plunder has operated solo more often than not. Selina understood early on that alibis are best kept by only one person. Partners in crime, while sometimes useful for complex capers, very often lose their sense of loyalty when faced with jail or an unequal cut of the profits. Cohorts can get you caught or dead… or *both*. So Catwoman prefers to act alone, teaming up with costumed criminals only as a last resort. At one time, before her conscience started to trouble her, the Feline Fatale wouldn't bat a whisker at consorting with the likes of Captain Cold, the Penguin, or Harley Quinn. But since changing her spots and trying harder to stay on the law-abiding side of the fence, Catwoman has become aware that running with rogues makes her appear guilty by *association*.

I'M MORELLA. THE *BIG* BOY IS SPIDER--AND THIS IS WIDOW ON MY LEFT.

Purring with the Penguin

When it pleases her, Selina has aligned herself with Gotham City "fixer" Oswald Cobblepot, a.k.a. the Penguin. Whether procuring information or bartering goods and services through Cobblepot's criminal underworld, Selina always makes sure she sits in the catbird seat when visiting the Penguin's Iceberg Lounge, a front for the crimelord's evil empire.

A POISONOUS PARTNERSHIP

Selina Kyle and beautiful botanist Pamela Isley have never really gotten along. Intruding like a weed on Catwoman's turf, Poison Ivy usually gives Selina cat-scratch fever. After Gotham's devastating earthquake, Catwoman prevented Ivy from sowing the city with fast-growing hyperseeds. Ivy repaid Catwoman by enslaving her with plant pheromones and making the Feline Fatale steal a $10 million ransom. In the end, Catwoman led Batman to Ivy's hideout for payback on the plant mistress.

TWO-TIMING TRICKSTER

Catwoman struck Manhattan with some stock market sleight-of-hand before she decided to run for Mayor of New York City. However, various enemies campaigned for Selina's downfall, enlisting the aid of the criminal Trickster to con Catwoman out of her ill-gotten gains!

Disguised as a prison guard, Harley helps Selina escape "rehabilitation."

Riot Girls

If the Clown Prince of Crime can't be trusted, the Joker's girlfriend—Harley Quinn—is even less likely to inspire Catwoman's confidence. Case in point: Harley manipulated Selina to make good their mutual escape from the rioting Cinque Rehabilitative Center. Harley used her psychological savvy to turn Catwoman into an unwitting and unwilling instrument of revenge against Commissioner Gordon for wronging both women!

HANGING WITH THE WRONG CROWD

Catwoman infiltrated S.P.I.D.E.R.—Society for Political Instability and Diverted Economic Resources—to loot the criminal cartel. After stealing her way into a secret underwater grotto near the French Riviera, the Feline Fatale was tapped by Morella, the group's leader, to head up its Theft division. Instead, Catwoman emptied the organization's coffers before destroying it from within.

Drugged by Harley, Catwoman held Gordon at gunpoint at the tomb of his late wife, Detective Sarah Essen Gordon.

Old flame Stark and tech-savvy Jeff rode a rocket with Selina to derail a Mafia money train.

SELINA'S BIG SCORE

Out of cash, Selina needed a major heist to get back on top. She assembled a crew to swipe $24 million from the Gotham mob, but she alone survived.

SUPER-HERO CATFIGHT

"Little birds should stay away from big bad kitty cats." Catwoman

CATWOMAN may have stolen Batman's heart, but his close allies prefer to keep their distance from the Feline Fatale. Dick Grayson, the first to take on the mantle of Robin the Boy Wonder, was excused from action during the more intimate moments when Batman interrogated Catwoman. Tim Drake, the current Robin, retains a deep distrust of Selina Kyle and isn't likely to sing her praises. As Batgirl, Barbara Gordon fought Catwoman in the past, but in her present information-gathering role as Oracle, Barbara has let bygones be bygones in order to take full advantage of Selina's skills. The Cat has also teamed with Oracle's super-hero associates, Black Canary and the Huntress, as an improbable, crime-fighting "Bird of Prey."

Catwoman has tangled with many a hero and heroine during her spectacular career straddling the line between good and not so good, including Superman, the Man of Steel himself.

Cat and Bird

"Once a thief, always a thief." At least that's what Robin believed when he discovered the Feline Fatale cavorting with the Dark Knight. Having tasted Catwoman's whip, the young hero was skeptical when Batman confessed his intentions to include Selina in his life. She didn't expect the Bat-Family to welcome her with open arms. But unbeknownst to her, Robin's antagonism had been carefully scripted by Batman himself to test Selina's trustworthiness.

Catwoman tussled with the Teen Wonder in the Batcave until Batman broke up the spat.

--AND I'LL CLIP YOUR WINGS.

NO MATTER WHAT YOUR "DADDY" SAYS.

Robin was sure that Catwoman had seduced Batman to find out his secret identity!

NIGHTWING

Dick Grayson, formerly Robin and now the hero Nightwing, understands that Batman and Catwoman are more than friends and less than enemies. Selina bristles when Nightwing tries to protect her, by turns flirting with him and fighting him.

When Batgirl daringly debuted as Gotham City's newest costumed crimefighter, Catwoman mistakenly assumed she was Batman's latest ladylove. This turned the Feline Fatale's eyes even *greener* with envy!

KISS AND RUN

Never having encountered the forward feline before, the Man of Steel was nonplussed when the purloining puss stole a kiss. He was so distracted she got clean away!

BIRD OF PREY

The Feline Fatale once joined Black Canary and the Huntress to stop the metahuman mercenary Braun, an amorous assassin who had wooed all three violent femmes. Later, the Cat and the Canary found themselves at odds on a hijacked prison train bound for the distant world of Apokolips.

Hunting the Huntress

Catwoman and that vengeful vigilante the Huntress both seek the Dark Knight's approval. But the Huntress does not suffer criminals lightly and looks on Catwoman as a common crook. The Gotham girls' roles were reversed when the Scarecrow's fear toxin turned the Huntress against Batman. Catwoman knocked some sense into Huntress in the *mother* of all catfights!

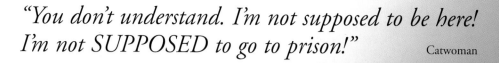

"You don't understand. I'm not supposed to be here! I'm not SUPPOSED to go to prison!"

Catwoman

CATWOMAN IN JAIL

Disorder in the Court

Surrounded by scores of cops, Catwoman was collared. Nevertheless, she refused to reveal her true identity. Fearing the prospect of prison, "Jane Doe" (as Selina renamed herself) pleaded guilty in exchange for reduced charges. But dodging state-penitentiary time still meant a two-year stretch at a private institution.

THE NIGHTMARE BEGINS...
To her dismay, Jane Doe was sent to the Cinque Foundation Rehabilitative Center. Its director, the evil Lea Norsling, relished the opportunity of breaking the new inmate's spirit.

TO CATCH A THIEF, a policeman has to *think* like a thief. And that's just what Commissioner James W. Gordon of the Gotham City Police Department did to finally cage the Catwoman. After Gotham had endured a cataclysmic earthquake and a year of nonstop crime, Gordon was determined to demonstrate beyond a shadow of doubt that law and order had prevailed. When the Princess of Plunder came home to the crime-weary city and committed daring new heists, Gordon decided to make an example of her as a warning to any other returning rogues who imagined Gotham to be easy meat. "Operation Catnip" was a carefully orchestrated trap laid at the Gotham City Museum of Art. Little did the Feline Fatale know that the priceless Egyptian statuette of the cat god Bast she had pilfered was bugged with a homing beacon that kept the bloodhounds of Gotham's Finest on her tail!

Center for Cruelty

The privately funded Cinque Center was established to rehabilitate first-time female offenders. Director Norsling described Cinque to Catwoman as a "learning institution," but "Jane Doe" knew that it was just another prison. Inmates were drugged to keep them quiet and sometimes even murdered as Norsling and her associates pocketed prison profits. Catwoman had to find a way out!

GET YOUR HANDS OFF ME! LET ME GO!

It took several of the Center's brutal guards to subdue desperate "Jane Doe."

I DON'T KNOW WHY I BOTHER WHEN--HEY! YOU ATE YOUR DIN--

--OOUPH!

DOCTOR HARLEEN QUINZEL

The jester's cap was a dead giveaway— Selina's rescuer was Harley Quinn!

Bad Girls Just Got Badder!

Brawling with her fellow "residents" landed Catwoman in solitary confinement. She was stripped and penned in a padded cell. Selina's thoughts turned to her past, crying out as she relived the traumas of her youth. In the next cell, resident Dr. Harleen Quinzel—a.k.a. Harley Quinn—listened intently to Selina's tragic story. When Catwoman overpowered her guard and ignited a riot, Harley Quinn escaped alongside Catwoman. Controlling Selina with drugs, Harley tried to make the Feline Fatale her catspaw and exact revenge on Commissioner Gordon!

YOU HAVE THE RIGHT TO REMAIN SILENT...

ACTUALLY, I'M HERE TO OFFER YOU A JOB.

BEAUTIFUL.

UNDERCOVER AGENT

A few years before her stay at the Cinque Center, Catwoman was arrested and transferred to the custody of a government agency headed by the no-nonsense Mr. Galiant. In exchange for complete immunity, Catwoman was forced to undertake several clandestine missions for "Dave," as she sarcastically dubbed Galiant. Catwoman's obedience was ensured by a satellite-controlled cyanide capsule implanted in her left bicep.

JUSTICE FOR ALL

Solving crimes hasn't exactly been what I'm famous for. But maybe I can see things that the police would NEVER notice.

Catwoman

SOMETIMES a different point of view is enough... Selina comforted herself with those very words as she hunted a homicidal monster in the dark alleyways of Gotham City. Returning to her old haunts after her criminal alter ego Catwoman had been presumed dead by the authorities, Selina knew her life was at a crossroads. She was plagued by insomnia as she struggled to figure out just who she was, with or without her cat mask. With the encouragement of her loyal ally Dr. Leslie Thompkins, Selina took a long look at herself trying to figure out where she had gone wrong in her life. When did Catwoman stop helping others and start just helping herself? When a frightened old friend walked through her door, Selina realized then and there that *someone* had to defend the defenseless from a heartless justice system—a system that showed no understanding for outsiders like herself. Selina resolved that, from now on, *Catwoman* would be that defender.

As teenagers, Selina Kyle and Rebecca Robinson were as thick as thieves. Rebecca even endured a knife-slashed cheek while defending Selina from a gang of bad boys. Years later, Selina returned the favor when Rebecca faced capital punishment for a murder she didn't commit!

THE ELEVENTH HOUR
On the eve of her execution by lethal injection, Rebecca's only chance lay with Catwoman, who planned a daring escape on the road to death row! After hijacking the prison van carrying Rebecca, Catwoman faked her friend's death so that she might start her life anew, just as Selina had done.

AN EYE FOR AN EYE IS MURDER!

AN EYE FOR AN EYE IS MURDER!

STOP THE KILLING

DEATH PEN CRUEL AND

Little did Selina realize that Batman watched over her every move while she rescued Rebecca.

STREET CRIME

In her youth, Selina Kyle snatched many a purse and picked many a pocket to get by. Her outlook has changed considerably since then. When a skateboard punk rolled away with Leslie Thompkins' purse, Selina showed her new policy of zero tolerance, humbling the skate-burglar with a well-aimed hubcap.

Bad Cop/Worse Cop

When Holly witnessed the murder of a narcotics agent by fellow G.C.P.D. lawmen, Catwoman was drawn into a complex web of police corruption, gem smuggling, and heroin dealing! The Feline Fatale worked with Detective Crispus Allen to save Holly's life from the crooked cops, and put $28 million in dirty diamonds to good use.

The spring-loaded crampons in Selina's boots make useful weapons.

Which is what I'm telling myself around nine that night as I nurse a drink in the diviest bar in the East End...

...dangling myself as bait for a killer.

Which is probably not the brightest idea I've ever had.

SO, uh... I HAVEN'T SEEN YOU IN HERE BEFORE, HAVE I?

I DON'T KNOW, MAYBE.

Sultry Selina's attempt at entrapment failed, but she caught the slayer's scent and trailed him back to his lair.

Serial Killer Stomped!

Someone or *something* was murdering the East End girls, crushing them to a bloody pulp. Selina became Catwoman again to prey on this perverted predator. Using herself as blonde bait, Selina went undercover and waited to be solicited by the slick serial killer, himself disguised to look like a handsome heartthrob! When Selina tracked him down, the shape-shifting monster got more than he bargained for!

NO!

CLAW BREAKERS

"I'm surprised you'd go to all this trouble. All I ever did was rob you."

Catwoman

CAT ON A HOT TIN ROOF

When a criminal with a grudge had Catwoman in her crosshairs, F.B.I. agents kept a watchful eye over the Feline Fatale.

Humiliated by Catwoman's repeated robberies, Toni Tiglon laid a trap for Catwoman with "help" from an undercover F.B.I. agent.

IF CATWOMAN had a nickel for every time someone has tried to kill her, she'd be a rich woman. Well, make that *richer*. But stealing from ruthless criminals like Antonia "Toni" Tiglon and plucking priceless gems from monstrous creatures like Gorilla Grodd has tested the Feline Fatale's powers of survival to their absolute limits.

As well as hired hitwomen hot on her tail, there are plenty of jealous copycats eager to mark Catty's turf as their own by putting her to sleep—permanently! And being the sultry sex kitten she is, Selina has attracted a string of psychopathic suitors who would rather see her dead than let her curl up with anyone else!

CURSE OF THE MUMMY

Hoping to snatch the Pendant of Bast, Catwoman awoke the "Grieving Undead," an Egyptian mummy who had been asleep for 4,796 years. The bandaged bachelor assumed she was his long-dead Egyptian love come back to life!

GORILLA GRODD

Grodd traded his simian soul to know the location of the Talisman of Arok, which would grant him dominion over Gorilla City. But the rightful king, Solovar, outmaneuvered Grodd by hiring Selina to steal the relic from the Mbutovillean embassy in East Africa. Grodd caught Catwoman, but she made chimp-change out of him!

Dangerous Curves

While running for mayor of New York City, Selina was encouraged to drop out or drop dead by a slew of stone killers. Blonde Bonny Hoffman and brunette Carmen Leno—the Body Doubles— were sent by the Requiem, Inc. assassination agency to terminate Selina's candidacy.

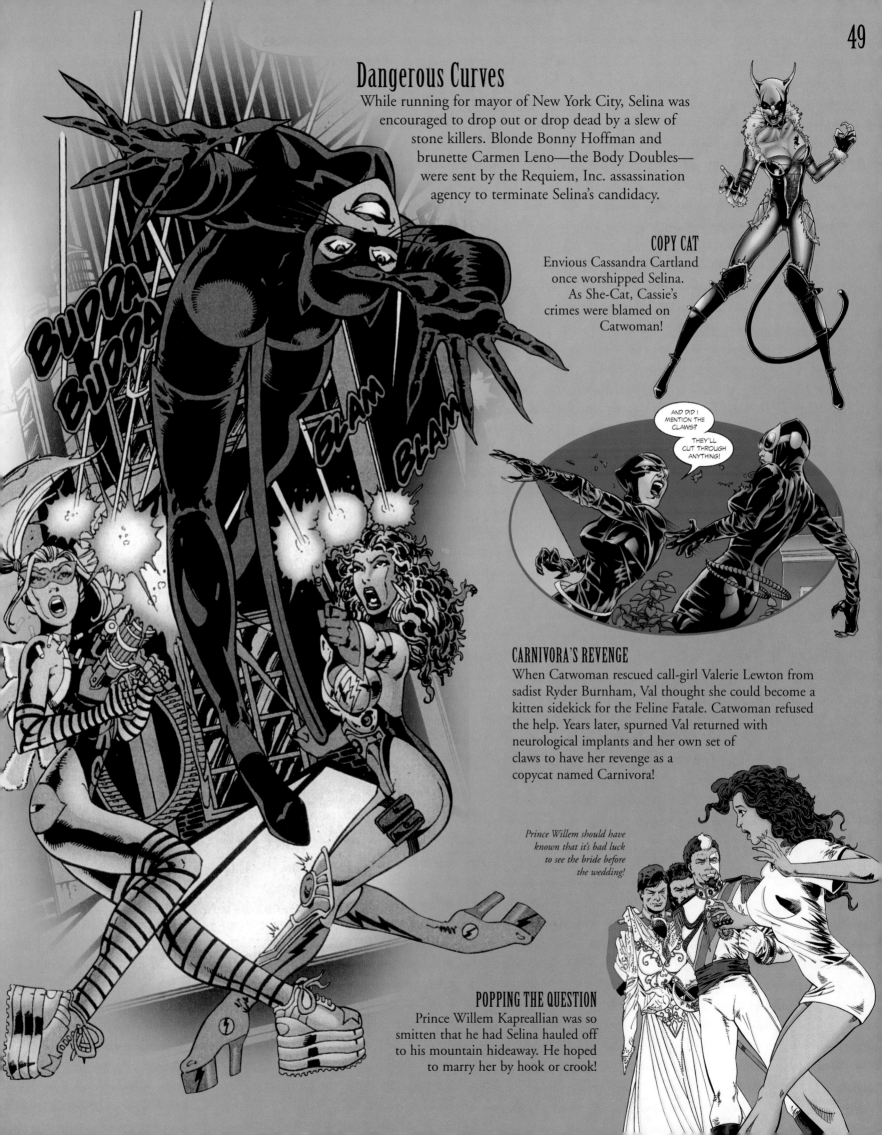

BUDDA BUDDA BUDDA

BLAM BLAM BLAM

COPY CAT
Envious Cassandra Cartland once worshipped Selina. As She-Cat, Cassie's crimes were blamed on Catwoman!

AND DID I MENTION THE CLAWS?

THEY'LL CUT THROUGH ANYTHING!

CARNIVORA'S REVENGE
When Catwoman rescued call-girl Valerie Lewton from sadist Ryder Burnham, Val thought she could become a kitten sidekick for the Feline Fatale. Catwoman refused the help. Years later, spurned Val returned with neurological implants and her own set of claws to have her revenge as a copycat named Carnivora!

Prince Willem should have known that it's bad luck to see the bride before the wedding!

POPPING THE QUESTION
Prince Willem Kapreallian was so smitten that he had Selina hauled off to his mountain hideaway. He hoped to marry her by hook or crook!

CAT HATERS

"Somebody must REALLY want me dead!"

Catwoman

CYBERC.A.T.

Christina Chiles wired the CyberC.A.T. robotic armor she developed for Syntex Systems Amalgamated to her own brain. But she still couldn't stop Catwoman making off with Syntex's top-secret technology!

Roman Sionis's ebony mask was burned onto his face in a fire.

ROGUES GALLERIES are usually reserved for heroes. Yet, although Catwoman may be a criminal, she still has a *conscience*. That's her near-fatal flaw! Selina routinely marks wealthy mob bosses like Black Mask for looting, making fools of them and adding some very, very dangerous enemies to her list. In addition, Catwoman has clashed with some of Batman's foes during her frequent team-ups with the Dark Knight. The Scarecrow delights in needling Selina's neuroses, while Poison Ivy has become both a persistent thorn in Selina's side as well as a romantic rival for the Bat himself! And if those weren't enemies enough, remorseless killers such as Lady Vic and Hellhound plot new ways to skin this Cat, either for reasons of business (the former) or pleasure (the latter).

POISON IVY

Professional rivalry or green-eyed envy? Catwoman and Poison Ivy—environmentalist turned eco-terrorist Pamela Isley—have a long-standing enmity, scratching with claws and thorns respectively each time they cross paths. Perhaps Ivy is jealous of Selina's ability to attract Batman without perfuming herself with mind-controlling plant pheromones.

Black Mask tortured to death Selina's brother-in-law, Simon Burton.

Sylvia used her personal knowledge of Selina to help Black Mask track Catwoman. Holly Robinson shot Sylvia to save one of Selina's nine lives.

BLACK MASK

With a fright mask carved from his father's coffin clamped to his face, Black Mask was the leader of Gotham's underworld. He had a dungeon to rival the Marquis de Sade's torture chambers and delighted in inflicting pain. When Catwoman's altruistic activities threatened his grip on Gotham's East End, the crazed crimelord enlisted the help of racketeer Sylvia Sinclair (right), a childhood chum of Selina's. Black Mask captured Catwoman, but she slipped out of his sadistic clutches and booted him off a rooftop, presumably to his death.

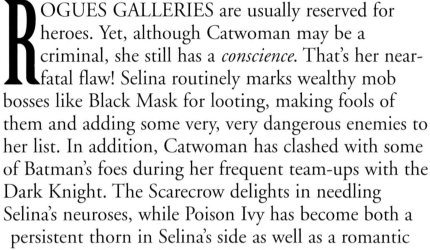

SCARECROW

Deranged Dr. Jonathan Crane has made a criminal career out of manipulating minds with his phobia-inducing Fear Gas. Sadly for Selina, Crane's alter ego, the Scarecrow, doesn't suffer from ailurophobia (a fear of cats)! On several occasions, Scarecrow has used the Feline Fatale as a panicked pawn to strike at the heart and mind of the Dark Knight, the man he fears most!

LADY VIC

To reclaim her family fortune, Lady Elaine Marsh-Morton markets herself as a merciless mercenary. She almost collected the bounty on Catwoman's head during Selina's mayoral bid by posing as demure Diane, a volunteer working for Selina's election campaign!

HELLHOUND

As martial-arts pupils, Selina and the arrogant Kai fought like cat and dog. Humiliated by Selina's skills, Kai became the killer Hellhound. He now believes his soul is in a state of flux and only by killing Catwoman can he be free!

CAREER of the CAT

I N "CAT YEARS" she would be 276 years old—but she doesn't look a single day over twenty-five! In the spring of 1940, operating as The Cat, she nearly stole the Dark Knight's thunder; in fact, the Caped Crusader was so smitten with her that he let her escape! In time, The Cat would become Catwoman. She would have black, blonde, or brunette tresses, depending on her mood. She would try to kiss Batman and, within a few pages, try to kill him, and he would make dogged attempts to reform her. The Princess of Plunder became the first Bat-Villainess to star in her own miniseries. Soon after, the first ongoing CATWOMAN comic book debuted. Today, Catwoman appears throughout the DC Comics Universe as a feline fixture who is constantly evolving, and continually clawing her way up everyone's Most Wanted list.

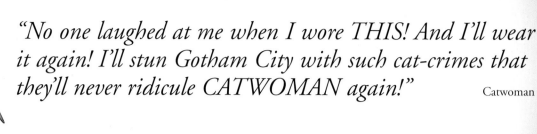

> *"No one laughed at me when I wore THIS! And I'll wear it again! I'll stun Gotham City with such cat-crimes that they'll never ridicule CATWOMAN again!"*
> Catwoman

STYLE CAT-ALOG

The Cat Creeps In...

By her third appearance in the Fall of 1940, The Cat began to answer to the sobriquet "Cat Woman." To complement her closet of dowager disguises, Selina donned a lifelike cat mask that could be folded away neatly in her purse. Topping off a high-priced silk evening gown and cloak in autumnal shades, Cat Woman could pass easily among Gotham City's fashionable elite and burgle their baubles!

WELL, WHAT'S THE MATTER?--HAVEN'T YOU EVER SEEN A PRETTY GIRL BEFORE?

BLACK CAT

Selina's 1942 "work clothes" made her over as a black cat in a crushed velvet dress with padded shoulders, accompanied by a magenta high-collared cloak, belt, and cuffed high-heeled boots. The "Cat-Woman" now donned clawed gloves—all the better to scratch out Batman's eyes for not noticing her!

SELINA KYLE'S FASHION SENSE has always been *finicky*. Like any feline, she is prone to primping and preening, especially where the signature costumes of her *style cat-alog* are concerned. But in the beginning, the celebrated jewel thief known as "The Cat" played dress-up in a variety of disguises to steal with stealth. The young, dark-haired beauty, who bedeviled Batman with her burglary, at first camouflaged her charisma by impersonating bent and wrinkled old women. In time, however, the feline fatale shed her frumpy frocks for a villainous vogue that fully embraced her role as the underworld's undisputed queen of crime, Catwoman! From cat-mask to cat-cowl to cat's-eye goggles, Selina has adapted her characteristic costumes to suit the times and keep pace with changing trends. However, while Catwoman's wardrobe has evolved over the years, she knows full well that *real* glamor and sensuality are *timeless* and effortlessly transcend the whims of fashion.

CLASSIC CATWOMAN

By 1947, Catwoman's costume evolved into a classy royal purple and green ensemble. Whether appearing as a Rogues Gallery member or a reformed malcontent, Selina could never be described as "retro" or "dated"—she was always the cat's meow!

Catwoman has worn both green and purple boots with this outfit.

Occasionally, Selina donned a gloveless version of this costume.

Cat's-eye bauble necklace

Catwoman accessorized this costume with a cat-shaped Catarang and a cat-compact filled with knockout powder instead of makeup!

Flaunt It !

Catwoman took her classic royal purple and green costume out of mothballs for much of the 1970s and 1980s. She briefly wore a monochromatic grey bodysuit in the late 1980s but returned to vamping it up in skintight violet spandex in the 1990s. Where she managed to stow stolen goods is a mystery!

Cat-o'-nine tails

Monochromatic sequined tights

Suede boots with three-inch heels

Thigh-high, stiletto-heeled leather boots

Going Green

Influenced by the Batman television series, Catwoman's 1967 catsuit emphasized her dangerous curves. Clad in iridescent emerald-green sequins with chartreuse accoutrements, Selina now adopted a cat's-eye domino mask with attached earpieces. She first modeled this look hoping to entice Batman into wedlock by joining him as a crook-catcher and renouncing her wicked ways!

NOW TO SWITCH ON MY LIGHT-INTENSIFIER CAT-GOGGLES!

Evening gloves gave Selina's 1969 look a vamplike air

TAKING THE PLUNGE

In 1969, the feline fatale wore a tail and proved she was no pussycat in a sexy, sleeveless ensemble with a plunging neckline, long satin gloves, and buckled, buccaneer boots. Selina cut her raven tresses into a short "flapper" bob, the first significant hairstyle change in decades!

In her first appearance, the Cat tempts the Bat to take a walk on the wild side!

CATWOMAN TIMELINE

IN BATMAN'S WORLD, she has always been the one that got away… and for good reason. Sometimes Catwoman eluded capture by her own design. But on more than one occasion, the Dark Knight actually allowed his nubile nemesis to escape justice… perhaps simply for the thrill of chasing her another night. The following chronology lists most of Catwoman's major appearances, her many flirtations with the Caped Crusader, and the countless adventures she has enjoyed on both sides of the law while living what may be MORE than nine lives over the past seven decades.

1940

Spring: **The Cat**, a fetching raven-haired jewel thief with a high-seas heist in mind, makes her debut in the premier issue of Batman's first self-titled comic book. (BATMAN #1)

Summer: Vying for the same stolen jewels, The Cat and the Joker first meet. But when the Clown Prince of Crime threatens to poison Batman's youthful partner Robin, The Cat offers up her ill-gotten gems to spare the Boy Wonder's life, thus revealing her aversion to killing. (BATMAN #2)

Fall: In her third appearance, The Cat appears in costume for the first time, sporting a fuzzy cat's-head mask. Sans costume (but fully clothed) The Cat later steals a kiss from Batman, stunning him while making good her escape. Later, she reveals her growing affection for the Caped Crusader. (BATMAN #3)

1942

April–May: The Cat officially becomes the **Catwoman**, now wearing a full-body black and magenta costume and masquerading as high society hostess **Marguerite Tone**. Once more, the Princess of Plunder bewitches Batman with a passionate kiss to elude capture. (BATMAN #10)

1943

February–March: Catwoman's real name (or one of them), **Elva Barr**, is revealed. When Bruce Wayne falls in love with the beautician Barr, his alter ego Batman offers her a second chance at redemption, later tripping up when he should be catching her. Catwoman, unfortunately, can't resist the lure of crime and is imprisoned by story's end. (BATMAN #15)

1944

April–May: In "The Duped Domestics!" a now-brunette Catwoman disguises herself as the beauteous **Belinda**, a maid who sweeps butler **Alfred Pennyworth** off his feet in order to rob Wayne Manor of its many treasures! (BATMAN #22)

1946

June–July: Batman faces a blonde Catwoman in "The Case Without a Crime!" The Feline Fatale dons an early short-sleeved version of her "classic" purple costume with cat-cowl and green cape. After a prison-escape facilitated by a hypnotizing cat's-eye jewel, her crimes begin to reflect cat icons and imagery. (BATMAN #23)

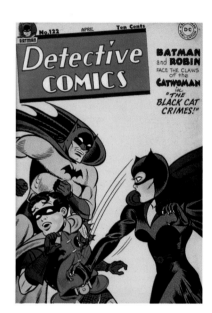

The Dynamic Duo may get top billing, but the Princess of Plunder will swipe at anyone who steals her spotlight!

Also this month, not only does Catwoman appear with red hair, she also attempts to murder Batman in her new labyrinthine lair, **The Cat-acombs!** Also, Catwoman's black cat pet **Hecate** is introduced. (BATMAN #35)

1947

February–March: Catwoman is first mentioned by name on a BATMAN comic book cover. In the tale contained therein, she first wields a cat-o'-nine-tails bullwhip concealed as her belt! (BATMAN #39)

April: Catwoman makes her first official cover appearance, giving Robin the Boy Wonder a scratching he won't soon forget! Catwoman's **Kitty-Car**, a high-powered speedster, is introduced. By story's end, Catwoman plunges the Kitty-Car off an open drawbridge to escape justice, thus leaving the Dynamic Duo to ponder whether or not she truly possesses nine lives like

On the cover of BATMAN #15, Catwoman pilots a flying cat to elude the Batplane!

her feline namesake. Beginning with this appearance, Catwoman is consistently portrayed with black hair, and her costume features a long-sleeved dress and (this issue only) "claw gloves." (DETECTIVE COMICS #122)

August–September: Robin helps Batman to peel back the cover of BATMAN #42 and reveal Catwoman slinking stealthily within its pages!

1948

February–March: When author Neil Weston omits Catwoman from *The Lady Rogues*, his book on history's greatest femme fatales, the Princess of Plunder schemes to prove herself the greatest villainess of all time! (BATMAN #45)

June–July: Disguised as **Madame Moderne**, Catwoman launches her own fashion magazine, *Damsel*, in "Fashions in Crime!" (BATMAN #47)

1951

December–January: The origin of Catwoman is first chronicled in "The Secret Life of the Catwoman!" As the story unfolds, Catwoman teams with the mysterious **Mister X** (in reality, a timid gunsel named Mousey) and later saves Batman from a collapsing building. Knocked unconscious herself, Catwoman awakens and reveals that she is actually **Selina Kyle**, once a stewardess for Speed Airlines and sole survivor of a plane crash that left her with amnesia and a penchant for purloining. Selina helps the Dynamic Duo to unmask Mister X and retires as Catwoman. (BATMAN #62)

June–July: Has Catwoman really retired? The Feline Fatale dons cape and cowl once again, but this time to help the Dynamic Duo harpoon crime czar **"Whale" Morton**. (BATMAN #65)

1952

February–March: Selina's brother Karl Kyle debuts as the first criminal "Catman," **The King of Cats!** (BATMAN #69)

1954

January: After being taunted by cheap crooks, pet shop proprietress Selina Kyle returns to a life of crime as Catwoman, first projecting a cat silhouette in the Gotham sky (just like the Bat-Signal), and then using her custom **Cat-apult** to launch an airborne heist of a mail helicopter! Catwoman also takes advantage of a woven-rope **cat's-cradle** rooftop bridge and pilots a getaway **Catboat**! (DETECTIVE COMICS #203)

Here she is, Miss Gotham! Catwoman forces the competition to take catnaps to prove herself the fairest of them all!

June: Catwoman attempts to alter the outcome of a beauty pageant in "The Sleeping Beauties of Gotham City!" (BATMAN #84)

September: After the raking retractor claws of her **Catplane** damage the Batplane and force it to land on a tropical isle, Catwoman's jungle cats hunt Batman and Robin! (DETECTIVE COMICS #211)

1963

January: Inspired by Catwoman's exploits, ex-big-game trapper Thomas Blake turns to villainy as **Cat-Man**, wielding razor-sharp Catarangs and swinging Catlines, and traveling in his customized Cat-Car and Catamaran! (DETECTIVE COMICS #311)

Bruce Wayne suggested to Thomas Blake that he should fight crime like Batman. But Blake had other plans…

1964

April: Once more a pet shop owner, Selina Kyle gives up her law-abiding (but boring) life to make mischief as Catwoman. But after her Catboat is found wrecked, the Dynamic Duo are unsure if the Princess of Plunder is living or dead! (BATMAN 80-PAGE GIANT #5)

1965

December: BATMAN #176 collects a Batman and Robin Sunday newspaper comic strip story detailing the Dynamic Duo's efforts to net Catwoman after she defies them to catch her in a nationwide chase beginning in Pittsburgh, Pennsylvania!

1966

January: The live-action *Batman* television series debuts, featuring Julie Newmar and Eartha Kitt portraying Catwoman during its two-year run.

November: Catwoman brainwashes intrepid reporter **Lois Lane** into assuming her criminal identity while the real Feline Fatale steals a kiss from Superman before turning him into a Superpussycat! (SUPERMAN'S GIRL FRIEND, LOIS LANE #70)

Elsewhere, Catwoman attempts to steal a young boy's alley cat, a kitten revealed to be a rare tailless Manx worth $5,000! (BATMAN KELLOGG'S SPECIAL)

Also this year, Catwoman—portrayed by Lee Meriwether—purrs onto the big screen as the popular *Batman* show leaps from television to feature film.

1967

November: Believing that Batgirl is "making a play for Batman," a jealous Selina Kyle declares her intentions to claim the Dark Knight as her own in the final page of DETECTIVE COMICS #369.

December: Catwoman adopts a green sequined catsuit and becomes a crook-catcher in an attempt to woo the Caped Crusader. (BATMAN #197)

Run, Robin, run! Or Catwoman's ferocious feline will make catfood out of you!

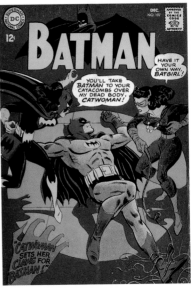

Hell hath no fury like a woman scorned… or a Feline Fatale finding out that there's a Batgirl *in the Batcave!*

Elsewhere this month, it's a case of mistaken identity when Batgirl and Supergirl undermine the heroics of Batman and Superman. The World's Finest team later discovers the super-heroines to be Catwoman and the Kandorian villainess **Black Flame** in disguise! And later still, Batman and Superman learn that the femme fatales aren't really female at all! They're actually the other-dimensional imps **Bat-Mite** and **Mr. Mxyzptlk**, magically transformed into vixens disguised as heroines. The gender-bending duo are having a bet to see if the Dark Knight will fall for their trap! (WORLD'S FINEST COMICS #169)

1969

March: At the Selina Slenderizing Salon, Catwoman dons an all-new costume and trains eight paroled lady criminals—including Light Laura, Florid Flo, Big Barbara, Sultry Sarah, Timid Trixie, and Leapin' Lena—to become her **Feline Furies**. This forces the Dynamic Duo to fight nine separate Catwomen! Also this issue, Selina Kyle's prison number (#102860) is revealed, and Catwoman utilizes her Light-Intensifier **Cat-Goggles** for the first time. (BATMAN #210)

Swinging samurai katanas, Catwoman and Diana Prince wage the mother of all catfights!

1972

May: It's the cat versus the canary as Catwoman takes on Black Canary in ADVENTURE COMICS #419!

July–August: After failing in her attempt to steal a cursed ruby known as the Fist of Flame, Catwoman finds herself in an unlikely alliance with Diana Prince, a.k.a. Wonder Woman! (WONDER WOMAN #201)

September–October: Catwoman and Diana Prince are transported to the magical land of Nehwon, where they team with **Fafhrd the Barbarian** and the **Gray Mouser** to fight the sorcerer Gawron and Lu Shan, treacherous daughter of Diana's martial-arts mentor I-Ching! (WONDER WOMAN #202)

1974

May–June: To free two rare albino tigers from the Tip-Top Circus, Catwoman disguises herself as the beauteous Nelias (an anagram of "Selina"), Queen of the Jungle Beasts. Unfortunately, a murder Catwoman

didn't commit draws the attention of the Dynamic Duo, who cage the Feline Fatale and nab the true culprit! This issue also features a look at Catwoman's different catsuits over the years. (BATMAN #256)

1975

August: Selina luckily escapes from a prison train and returns to crime as Catwoman, wearing her purple costume once more. (BATMAN #266)

1976

September–October: In the final issue of the Joker's brief comic-book series, Catwoman and the Clown Prince of Crime are outsmarted by movie clown Benny Springer and his famous cat co-star Hiawatha. (THE JOKER #9)

November–December: In his first full-length adventure, Robin comes up against **Catgirl**! Catwoman doesn't take kindly to the young upstart, and tries—but fails—to target the million-dollar kitty in **"Motown" Nathan's** poker game at Gotham's Kit-Kat Club. (BATMAN FAMILY #8)

December: Batman and Wonder Woman unite to capture Catwoman, who renounces her U.S. citizenship to become Ambassadress of Sudaria after sending a pair of jaguars to kill the previous envoy! True to form, by story's end Catwoman vanishes before the Dark Knight and the Amazon Princess can cage her. (THE BRAVE AND THE BOLD #131)

Holy copycats, Batman! The Boy Wonder uses his Batline to weave a cat's cradle to catch the mysterious Catgirl!

1977

September: When Batman is presumed murdered, Catwoman gives her version of what really happened to the Caped Crusader! (BATMAN #291)

November–December: On Earth-2, a parallel Earth featuring "Golden Age" versions of DC characters, Bruce Wayne and Selina are married! The birth of their daughter, Helena, and Catwoman's demise are recounted in a tale featuring Helena's debut as **The Huntress**! (DC SUPER-STARS #17)

1978

November–December: Batgirl, Batwoman, and Earth-2's Huntress unite to defeat Earth-1's Catwoman, Poison Ivy, and **Madame Zodiac**. (BATMAN FAMILY #17)

1979

April: Having given up her wicked ways (again), Selina Kyle asks Bruce Wayne to go on a date with her. (BATMAN #310)

July: Selina Kyle enjoys a night on the town with Bruce Wayne, never realizing that her billionaire beau is really the Batman! Sadly, Selina's romance with Bruce is short-lived. (BATMAN #313)

December: Selina begins having headaches that portend a possible end to her nine lives. (BATMAN #318)

1980

April: Selina learns that she suffers from a rare disease that could end her life at any moment! (BATMAN #322)

May: When the Egyptian Cat-God Exhibition is stolen from Gotham City's Riverside Museum, Batman believes Selina Kyle has returned to crime. To prove her innocence, Selina takes up her Catwoman costume anew and discovers that Cat-Man is to blame! (BATMAN #323)

Don't have kittens, Batman! The Dark Knight finds himself caught in a litter of nine clawing Catwomen!

June: Batman takes a wounded Catwoman back to his Batcave for the first time, where he learns of her mysterious malady. After a battle with Cat-Man—who is apparently parboiled alive in a geyser—Catwoman's disease goes into complete remission. This was perhaps a result of clutching Cat-Man's magical cloak which purportedly gives its wearer nine lives… or in Selina's case, nine more. (BATMAN #324)

Catwoman was literally dying *to see Batman's secret underground headquarters, the Batcave!*

August: Selina and Bruce call off their romance (for now). (BATMAN #326)

1981

February: Catwoman appears in her first solo tale, a back-up feature beginning in the pages of BATMAN #332. Meanwhile, the issue's lead story begins the four-part "Lazarus Affair," pitting Batman, Robin, Catwoman, and government agent King Faraday against Rā's al Ghūl. Catwoman meets Talia, Rā's's daughter, competition for the Dark Knight's affections.

October: In a retro-tale set on Earth-2, Selina Kyle's wedding to Bruce Wayne is witnessed by guests Lois Lane and Clark Kent, a.k.a. Superman! (SUPERMAN FAMILY #211)

1982

June: In a two-part tale, Catwoman is hired to protect presidential candidate Daniel Brown from death threats later revealed to be from Brown's wife Janice and his running mate Peter Simmons. (BATMAN #348)

August: After finding the dead body of stripper **Candy Carole**, Selina impersonates Candy to solve her murder. (BATMAN #350)

1983

January: A jealous, unhinged Catwoman targets Bruce Wayne's latest love **Vicki Vale** for extermination, leading Batman to confront the Feline Fatale and end their relationship once and for all. (BATMAN #355)

1984

April: In "The Autobiography of Bruce Wayne," Earth-2's Batman reflects on the adventure teaming Catwoman and himself to defeat the Scarecrow, a pairing that would eventually lead to their marriage. (THE BRAVE AND THE BOLD #197)

1985

April: Though not a major player in DC Comics' mammoth CRISIS ON INFINITE EARTHS 12-issue maxiseries, Catwoman's history is significantly altered as a result of this continuity-razing storyline which combines all of DC's "Earths" into a single world with one timeline. Since Earth-2 no longer exists, Batman and Catwoman were never married, and thus, never sired Helena Wayne (a.k.a. The Huntress). (CRISIS ON INFINITE EARTHS #1)

1986

February: With the Boy Wonder grown up and away from the roost, Batman and Catwoman form a dynamic duo of their own beginning in BATMAN #392, a yearlong teaming of this crime-fighting couple that continues through the pages of BATMAN and DETECTIVE COMICS.

It's a nightmare at the movies when Catwoman and Batman see the Film Freak's feature presentation!

March: Selina Kyle is a featured player in BATMAN: THE DARK KNIGHT RETURNS, writer/artist Frank Miller's acclaimed graphic novel featuring a Caped Crusader forced out of retirement to confront old and new villains in an apocalyptic near-future.

May: Catwoman aids Batman as he faces the **Film Freak**! (DETECTIVE COMICS #562)

1987

February: The Dark Knight's origin is updated during the four-part "Batman: Year One" storyline chronicling the Caped Crusader's first forays into crime-fighting. Selina Kyle appears as a Gotham City prostitute tiring of the oppression she sees around her. Selina's fellow prostitute **Holly "Gonightly" Robinson** appears. (BATMAN #404)

May: Selina dons her catsuit for the first time (again) as Catwoman! (BATMAN #407)

December: To break up the "Dynamic Trio" of Batman, Robin, and a reformed Catwoman, the Joker abducts the Princess of Plunder and "reprograms" her to evil with the aid of the diabolical **Dr. Moon** and his altered catscan device! (DETECTIVE COMICS #569)

1988

August: Catwoman begins a four-part tale in DC Comics' then-weekly ACTION COMICS anthology. Holly is killed in ACTION COMICS #613. However, her demise is not permanent. (ACTION COMICS #611-614)

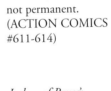

Jealous of Bruce's flirtation with Vicki Vale, Selina vents her feelings to her pet panther, Diablo.

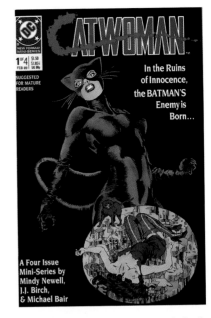

Catwoman's debut miniseries spotlighted her history with Ted Grant (Wildcat) and introduced her sister Maggie.

1989

February: Catwoman's origin is revamped in her own four-issue miniseries, the first solo title for the Feline Fatale. (CATWOMAN #1)

November: Catwoman is serialized in the *St. Louis Dispatch* newspaper, a comic strip running until January 1990.

1991

March: "Sisters In Arms," a two-part tale, begins this month in BATMAN #460 and features Catwoman crossing paths with G.C.P.D. **Sgt. Sarah Essen** and reporter Vicki Vale.

DAMN HER.

1992

June: DC Comics' adapts the blockbuster movie *Batman Returns* (with Michelle Pfeiffer as Selina Kyle). (BATMAN RETURNS)

Also this year, Catwoman appears in CATWOMAN DEFIANT, the first graphic novel to feature the Princess of Plunder. Batman enlists her help in stopping the beauty-destroying **Mister Handsome** and his **Model Army**.

CATWOMAN #0 revealed that Selina was forced to steal as an orphan. She sharpened her skills in the backstreet slums of Gotham City.

1993

January: Catwoman headlines the first four issues of DC Comics' SHOWCASE '93 anthology.

June: As the four-part "Heat" begins in the pages of LEGENDS OF THE DARK KNIGHT #46, Catwoman joins with Batman to defeat **Cat-man**.

August: Finally! Catwoman's first-ever comic-book series debuts with the Princess of Plunder forced to ply her trade for the terrorist **Bane**. Catwoman's fence **Leopold** first appears. (CATWOMAN #1)

1994

January: Catwoman is the first to realize that Batman, injured by Bane, has been replaced by Jean Paul Valley, a.k.a. **Azrael**. (BATMAN #503)

March: Selina Kyle's butler **Wilder** appears. (CATWOMAN #8)

August: Selina's trusted chauffeur **Caleb** makes his one and only appearance to date. (CATWOMAN #13)

October: Catwoman's origin is retold, including the death of her alcoholic father and her childhood at the Seagate Juvenile Home for Girls (later renamed Sprang Hall). (CATWOMAN #0)

November: Selina is forced to work for a shadowy government agency led by the ruthless **"Dave" Galiant**. A remote-operated cyanide capsule implanted in her arm ensures her cooperation. (CATWOMAN #15)

Elsewhere, in the "Elseworlds" BATMAN: BLOODSTORM, the bite of a vampire turns Selina Kyle into a half-cat/half-human being.

1995

February: Selina escapes marriage to **Prince Willem Kapreallian** of Transbelvia and manages to extract Galiant's subcutaneous cyanide capsule. (CATWOMAN #18)

March: Catwoman blackmails Galiant with Nazi secrets to escape his leash. (CATWOMAN #19)

April: On the tropical movie set of *Lethal Honey III*, Catwoman crosses paths with the **Lurker**, a special effect gone awry! (CATWOMAN #20)

July: CATWOMAN ANNUAL #2 reveals that Selina and the assassin **Hellhound** trained together under the tutelage of the **Sensei**.

October: With Robin, Catwoman meets the high-tech hacker thieves known as the **Psyba-Rats**. (CATWOMAN #25)

1996

January: Selina teams with villains **Slyfox**, **Giz**, **Mouse**, and **Steeljacket** for a series of heists planned by lawyer **Troy Cavanaugh**. (CATWOMAN #28)

February: Catwoman is one of the major players in DC VERSUS MARVEL COMICS, a four-issue miniseries pitting major characters from their comic-book companies in a race to save both universes from destruction!

March–April: During the "Contagion" storyline in Batman titles, Catwoman helps the Dark Knight and his allies to find a cure for "The Clench," a plague decimating Gotham City's populace. (CATWOMAN #31-32)

April: In the "Amalgam Universe" of heroes and villains, Catwoman is blended with the lethal lady **Elektra** to become the samurai-sword-wielding bombshell known as **Catsai**! (ASSASSINS #1)

In BATMAN: BLOODSTORM, were-cat Selina Kyle gives her life to save her beloved Batman by leaping into the path of a crossbow bolt meant to pierce his vampire heart!

May: Catwoman crosses paths with Hellhound for the first time since their teen years. (CATWOMAN #33)

September: Catwoman becomes a reluctant "Bird of Prey" when she teams with the **Black Canary** and the Huntress within the four-issue BIRDS OF PREY: MANHUNT miniseries.

October: The three-part "Year Two" storyline begins; Selina "steals" the Joker, Penguin, and Two-Face from custody. She then helps Batman recapture them. (CATWOMAN #38)

1997

January: Detective **Moreland McShane** is assigned by **Commissioner Gordon** to track down Catwoman, who scars Moreland's cheeks with her claws. (CATWOMAN #41)

February: Catwoman joins bloodsucking femme fatale **Vampirella** to snare a were-cat in the first crossover between DC Comics and Harris Comics. (CATWOMAN / VAMPIRELLA: THE FURIES)

'Til death do them part? Not even! After robbing an Egyptian tomb, Catwoman uncovers a mummy with attitude!

Also this month, Selina meets dwarfish criminal fixer **Zee**, copycat thief **She-Cat** and the armored **CyberC.A.T.**! (CATWOMAN #42)

April: Selina and Bruce enjoy a Valentine's Day date. (BATMAN: THE LONG HALLOWEEN #5)

Also this month, She-Cat is revealed to be **Cassandra Cartland**, an orphan who knew Selina at Seagate. (CATWOMAN #44)

August: Selina crosses **Morella** and her criminal organization **S.P.I.D.E.R.**! (CATWOMAN #48)

October: In CATWOMAN's 50th issue, Selina dons cybernetic armor to defeat the returned CyberC.A.T.

November: Catwoman sharpens her claws alongside the vampire **Scream Queen** in CATWOMAN PLUS... #1.

December: Moreland McShane discovers Selina's secret identity... and Selina learns that McShane is "The Headhunter," a serial killer! (CATWOMAN #53)

Elsewhere, in "I Married a Mummy," Catwoman inadvertently unleashes an undead Egyptian pharaoh determined to make the Princess of Plunder his bride! (CATWOMAN ANNUAL #4)

1998

April: Disguised as Metropolis reporter **Cat Grant**, Catwoman infiltrates the

JLA Watchtower and helps the super-team defeat the diabolical Prometheus. (JLA #17)

Also this month, when Gotham City is hit by an earthquake, Catwoman saves victims trapped in the rubble. (CATWOMAN #56)

August: Selina reunites with boxing coach **Ted Grant**, a.k.a. **Wildcat**, in the four-issue CATWOMAN/WILDCAT miniseries beginning this month.

November: During DC Comics' centuries-spanning ONE MILLION crossover, a time-traveling Batman meets the Catwoman of the 853rd century! (CATWOMAN #1,000,000)

1999

March: Leaving devastated Gotham, Catwoman relocates to Manhattan. After breaking into the Louvre and stealing a shield once carried by Joan of Arc, she meets French felon **Blackmont**! (CATWOMAN #66)

May: In her attempt to "steal" New York, Selina Kyle runs for mayor and is targeted by assassins **Gunhawk**, **Lady Vic**, and the **Body Doubles**. Catwoman now wears a purple catsuit. (CATWOMAN #68)

August: Selina returns to Gotham City, now a lawless No Man's Land. (CATWOMAN #71)

September: To show that he needs Catwoman's help to secure information crucial to reclaiming Gotham, Batman kisses her. (CATWOMAN #72)

October: Attempting to steal the computer discs Batman needs, Catwoman tangles with security experts **Hardcases, Inc.** (CATWOMAN #73)

November: Selina is shot and left for dead by Lex Luthor's bodyguard **Mercy**. (CATWOMAN #74)

December: More secrets of Selina's childhood are revealed as a wounded Catwoman recalls her time learning sleight-of-hand from carnival hustler **Del Halperm**. (CATWOMAN #75)

Also this year, in the two-part "Elseworlds" miniseries CATWOMAN: GUARDIAN OF GOTHAM, Bruce Wayne "creates" Catwoman by murdering her parents. Selina marries Bruce and discovers that he is really the evil killer known as Batman!

2000

March: As Gotham City rebuilds, Selina Kyle establishes a new residence, and lets the city know that Catwoman is back with a daring heist! (CATWOMAN #78)

April: A trap laid by Commissioner Gordon leads to Catwoman's capture. She is sentenced to two years at the Cinque Foundation Rehabilitative Center. (CATWOMAN #79)

June: In solitary at the Cinque Center, Selina recalls her mother's suicide and her younger sister **Maggie**. (CATWOMAN #81)

July: Fellow femme fatale **Harley Quinn** helps Selina break out of jail. (CATWOMAN #82)

September: Harley Quinn and Catwoman take Commissioner Gordon hostage. Batman frees Gordon, but Catwoman and Harley escape. (CATWOMAN #84)

November: Catwoman wears a new stylish costume: hip-hugging leather pants, bustier, jacket, and domino mask. (CATWOMAN #86)

2001

January: The five-part "Terror" story begins; Catwoman and Batman declare a truce to defeat the diabolical duo of **Professor Hugo Strange** and the Scarecrow. (BATMAN: LEGENDS OF THE DARK KNIGHT #137)

March: Commissioner Gordon is gunned down, and the Bat-Family—Nightwing, Robin, Azrael, and Batgirl—suspect Selina! (CATWOMAN #90)

July: After 96 issues—including CATWOMAN #0 and CATWOMAN #1,000,000—the Feline Fatale is apparently slain by **Deathstroke**. So ends her first comic-book run. (CATWOMAN #94)

August: Private eye **Slam Bradley** is hired by the Mayor of Gotham City to establish whether Catwoman is alive or dead. He finds Selina very much alive, but she persuades him to destroy his files and keep her existence secret. (DETECTIVE COMICS #759)

2002

January: Catwoman's second comic-book series debuts with a new look for the Feline Fatale. She is now resolved to help the downtrodden of Gotham City, and investigates the murders of several prostitutes. Slam Bradley

becomes a major player in Selina's life and her friend Holly returns. (CATWOMAN *vol. 2* #1)

April: Catwoman captures the shape-changing prostitute killer and turns him over to Batman. CATWOMAN *vol. 2* #4)

Everything a cat-fancier needs to know can be found within the pages of CATWOMAN SECRET FILES, including why Holly Robinson is alive!

September: Catwoman incites the ire of Gotham crimelord **Black Mask**, who will become an ongoing threat to her and her nearest and dearest. (CATWOMAN *vol. 2* #9)

November: Further details of Catwoman's secret life are revealed in CATWOMAN SECRET FILES AND ORIGINS #1.

December: More details of Selina's youth are revealed, including her friend **Sylvia**, who once worked with Selina for the malicious **Mama Fortuna**. Sylvia now watches over a gang of kid thieves and has secret ties to Black Mask. Meanwhile, Slam Bradley tells Holly of his romantic interest in Selina. (CATWOMAN *vol. 2* #12)

Also this year, Selina's desperation for fast cash leads to a daring robbery of a train carrying mob money in the graphic novel CATWOMAN: SELINA'S BIG SCORE.

2003

April: To save an abducted Holly, Catwoman confronts Black Mask and Sylvia. In the

ensuing conflict, Black Mask seemingly falls to his death while Sylvia is shot dead by Holly. (CATWOMAN *vol. 2* #16)

August: Selina reunites with Ted Grant (Wildcat), who teaches Holly some of his hard-hitting techniques before teaming with Catwoman for a late-night romp against religious zealots. (CATWOMAN *vol. 2* #20)

September: On vacation in Keystone City, Catwoman joins **Captain Cold**—a member of the Flash's Rogues Gallery—to steal the original Scarlet Speedster's helmet from the Keystone City Time Capsule Memorial. The Feline Fatale secretly plans to return the helmet to its rightful owner. (CATWOMAN *vol. 2* #23)

November: Catwoman journeys to Opal City, home of **Starman**! (CATWOMAN *vol. 2* #23)

Also this year, BIRDS OF PREY: BATGIRL/CATWOMAN #1 and BIRDS OF PREY: CATWOMAN/ORACLE #2 link past to present as Selina Kyle and Barbara Gordon team to stop **Valerie Lewton**, a catsuit-wearing killer anxious to take Catwoman's place in Gotham's underworld!

On the trail of Holly's long-lost brother, Selina hits the heights in Opal City, home of the hero Starman.

INDEX